Pra

The Key To LIFE: *Li* ... *Expression*

"If you are on a journey to Self recovery, you may have an idea of where you want to go … yet find yourself at a loss as to how to get there. Jim Phillips' book, *The Key to LIFE: Living in Full Expression* is the guidebook you've been looking for. *The Key to LIFE* is filled with practical wisdom and anecdotes. It will open your mind to new ways of looking at life and, more importantly, your Self. Prepare to discover the truth of who you are! This is a book you will want to refer to time and time again. I highly recommend it to everyone who is on their spiritual journey."

~ Robin Jay, Award-winning Author and Filmmaker,
Motivational Speaker

"*The Key to LIFE: Living In Full Expression* is a thought provoking guide to exploring, expressing and experiencing the Truth of who we are. As Jim Phillips says, "there is no right path or wrong path, there is your path." He eases you down your path to greater awareness, with simply stated wisdom. I recommend it to anyone looking for a more fulfilling, rewarding experience of life and Self."

~ Mary McDonough, Actor, Award-winning Filmmaker, Bestselling Author of *Lessons from the Mountain*, *What I learned from Erin Walton*

"Jim has written a wonderful book! He has the heart of a mystic and the mind of a scholar. I love *The Key To LIFE* because of its essence rooted in divine love. However, the practical ideas are presented in a grounded fashion that is easy for the logical mind to follow. This book is filled with timeless wisdom that seems brand new because of Jim's

unique anecdotes and catch phrases. Balanced and beautiful, I highly recommend *The Key to LIFE*."
~ Tara L. Robinson, Hay House Author of *The Ultimate Risk*

"Jim Phillips has written the owner's manual to living your best life. His ability to present complex spiritual concepts in a practical and common sense way is impressive. You'll find wisdom on every page. Highly recommended!"
~ Irene Kendig, International Award-Winning Author of *Conversations with Jerry and Other People I Thought Were Dead*

"Jim Phillips has shared steps of simplicity and truth in his book, *The Key to LIFE: Living In Full Expression*. Within it, find your treasure and in doing so, your key."
~ Simran Singh, Award-winning Author of *Conversations with the Universe and Your Journey to Love*, Founder of *11:11 Magazine*

The Key to LIFE

The Key to LIFE

Living in Full Expression

Ancient wisdom for a modern world

Jim Phillips

The information provided in this book is designed to provide helpful information on the subjects discussed. This book is not meant to be used, nor should it be used, to diagnose or treat any medical condition. The author and publisher are not responsible for any specific health needs that may require medical supervision and are not liable for any damages or negative consequences from any treatment, action, application, or preparation, to any person reading or following the information in this book.

References are provided for information purposes only and do not constitute endorsement of any websites or other sources. In the event you use any of the information in this book for yourself, the author and the publisher assume no responsibility for your actions.

Books may be purchased through booksellers or by contacting Sacred Stories Publishing.

The Key to LIFE: Living In Full Expression
2nd Edition
Jim Phillips
Tradepaper ISBN: 978-1-945026-25-6
Electronic ISBN: 978-1-945026-26-3

Library of Congress Control Number: 2016958934

Published by Sacred Stories Publishing
Delray Beach, FL
www.sacredstoriespublishing.com

Printed in the United States of America

Table of Contents

"To all who have accompanied me on this souljourn and played their role brilliantly so that I might live in full expression."

"It is in our living in full expression
that the Divine is fully expressed."
Jim Phillips

Foreword

In the years that I have known him, I have persistently encouraged Jim to write a book. I am, therefore, very excited that he has dedicated the time and energy to accomplish this task. I know that I, and many others, will benefit greatly from what he has written.

I first met Jim when he came to me as a client in my Intuitive Coaching practice. My unique approach is to use my intuition to connect with a client's Soul and convey to them their soul's purposes for their life as well as guidance from that level of their being. From the very first session with Jim I could see that he is one of those people whose soul has chosen to be of service in this world, to share his insights and wisdom to uplift and empower others. Jim has done an outstanding job of this as a lecturer, life coach and an author.

Jim is well-spoken and able to form analogies for spiritual truths that make them accessible for everyone in a very practical way. I have seen people's eyes open wide in response to a simple statement he made because it so neatly brought them to a deeper understanding of how they could change and improve their lives in an immediate sense, not some far-off and longed-for time in the future. His confidence in each person's capacity to create in their lives and experience true happiness is inspiring and energizing. His ability to listen with compassion and without judgment creates a reassuring presence for everyone. I know that all of what I am describing has also been perceptibly conveyed in this book. Prepare to be surprised, affirmed, and enlightened by what you read.

In the first early minutes of each day, Jim has been taking walks and contemplating life. During these quiet and often beautiful walks it became apparent to him that many of his questions about life and the Divine were being answered and wisdom from a higher source was being conveyed to him. This is something that we are all capable of experiencing, and Jim would be the first one to agree. I am grateful that he took the time and had the discipline to write down what he was receiving. At first his intention was to merely record the Truths for himself, to read over and process for his personal and spiritual growth. Eventually, as the material increased, he decided to share it with others, first in workshops and now in book form. I am very grateful he made that choice.

You have in your hands a book that you will want to read more than once. It is the kind of book that you can open to any page and be touched by its content. It has been written through an openness to Spirit and all that is good in the world. I know it will be a blessing for you and for all of us. Enjoy!

Christen McCormack
Founder
Spirit School of the Intuitive Arts

Preface

From the Beginning

It was in the fall of 1967 that I had an experience that would forge the course of my life. At the time, I didn't understand the impact this event would have on my life or how it would play out. However, in hindsight I see how the experience, which was seeded in my subconscious mind, created opportunities for me to fulfill its promise.

I was sitting in church one Sunday morning taking in all that was happening around me. The minister was speaking and inviting all to contribute what they could as the offering basket was passed among the congregation. As I observed what was taking place a feeling came over me that something was not quite right. It wasn't that anything was wrong so much as it just wasn't quite right. At the age of thirteen I had no idea why I was having this feeling and certainly no idea of the impact that what was to follow would have on my life's journey.

As I sat there trying to understand the thoughts and feelings I was experiencing a clear voice said, "You will be doing this one day." Somewhat startled I looked around to determine the source of the voice but it was not to be found. *Doing what?* I thought. Being a minister in a church? There is no way. It wasn't because I had anything against the church or being a minister; it just didn't feel right to me. I was raised a Christian, believed in God, and yet something was a little off. And then that same calm, clear voice said, "You will be doing it differently."

And so it is forty-five or so years later that I find myself sharing what I have come to know and understand about spirituality, life, and our purpose. I guess you could say that what I do through my coaching, writing, and speaking is like what a minister does, only different.

The writing of this book is the culmination of years of self-reflection, study and life experiences. It is by no means to be taken as an absolute on how life is, how life should be or how life will unfold from this moment forward. It is intended to give you a perspective on what is possible when you know and accept who you are, why you are here and what you are capable of creating and experiencing. There is nothing you cannot experience when you give your Self permission to live in full expression of the truth of who you are.

Housekeeping

A few final notes before we begin this shared experience of our respective life's journeys. You will read many phrases that are shown in this book as quotes. You have in fact already read some. Most of the phrases were given to me either during my meditations or in periods of deep reflection and contemplation.

I use several words in this book to identify that which I know as and refer to as God. You will see the words God, Spirit, the Universe and the Divine used. If none of these words resonate with you simply replace them with what is appropriate for you and your beliefs.

Throughout this book when you see the word "Self" capitalized it signifies that higher aspect of each one of us. It is the integration of our human spirit with our Divine Spirit that desires to be experienced and expressed.

Your will find the use of a word, souljourn, that I created to describe each lifetime on Earth. It is the combination of the words Soul and sojourn. The word *sojourn* as we find it in any dictionary is defined as a short or temporary stay. When we combine the word sojourn with Soul, that aspect of us that is the Divine, we get souljourn: a short or temporary stay in a place (Earth) as that aspect of the Divine that is here to express, experience, and expand upon itself through the experiences we call life.

Enjoy your souljourn. You chose to be here at this time and place. Live in full expression of who you know yourself to be in every moment and aspect of your life. You are the love and joy you so strongly desire to experience and express. You are the difference you desire to see and experience in the world.

"For these times are tenuous times, more so than any human being has known throughout the centuries. It is in these tenuous times the foundation and cornerstones that can be laid are that of the Human Spirit returning again to its own Divine sources and these combined realizations. The realization of the importance of the Human Spirit, and the realization of the importance of the Divine Spirit, working together and creating together a world which can hold Peace and Peacefulness."

Yeshua

Introduction

The Time Has Come

When I first wrote and released *The Key to LIFE, Living In Full Expression*, I did so out of a sense of urgency. There was a strong desire to get the book completed because I felt as though I had procrastinated long enough. What I came to realize however is that it was not complete. There was more I was to experience about my Self and life that were to be a part of what you now hold in your hands. The process was difficult at times but only because I chose for it to be. I experienced many of the simplexities of life which I now have the opportunity to share with you.

The majority of the original introduction has been left intact as it was when the book first appeared. It offers a general understanding of how and why the book came to be and what it offers to you. I trust you will enjoy this exploration of whom you are and why you are here as you live in full expression of that truth.

The message of this book has been patiently waiting to be expressed for quite some time—years, in fact. Maybe it didn't come forward, because I wasn't ready. Maybe there were more experiences I was to have so that what I wrote would make sense from an experiential point of view. Maybe the time wasn't right for those who would receive the ideas and thoughts to be shared. Quite frankly, it is all of the above. I have had many experiences that allowed me to better understand the information that I was being given to share. This doesn't mean my life has been any different from anyone else's—quite the contrary. I believe it has been quite normal with its share of successes, disappointments, challenges, and victories. There have been a few experiences most people might not have had, some of which will be shared in this book, but all in all my life has been quite normal.

I have information that I believe was given to me to share. Some of the information comes while taking early morning walks when all is still and quiet. There are no distractions other than a gentle breeze, an occasional jogger and the early morning calls of the various birds I encounter. I have come to call these early morning experiences, *being immersed in the silence of the dawn,* a time when I am most receptive to the information that somehow finds its way into my awareness. It could be an answer to a question I pose as I begin my walk, a solution to a challenging experience I am in the midst of or simply information I am intended to receive.

In essence it is a walking meditation, a time during which I receive guidance from my higher source. Over the years what I have come to understand is that the guidance is and always has been there for me, just as it is and always has been available to you through your higher source. It took time however to trust in that source to the point that I now accept and know that it will never lead me astray.

This book was not written because I think I have the answers. It was written because I think what I know and have experienced can be of benefit as you consider your life: where you are, where you would like to be, and perhaps more importantly, who you are, why you are here and what you are here to create.

What I have written is the truth as I know it at the time of writing. I am not suggesting that you believe what you read, just be open and receptive to a perspective that until now you might not have considered. I can assure you that what I know and accept as true in this moment will change as we continue along our respective path of understanding, experience, expression and expansion.

"What I believe does not change the Truth, however, the Truth can change what I believe."

This book is about expressing, experiencing, and accepting our Self as we are: fully, completely and wholly (holy). It is the expression and experience of the sacred relationship with our Self through appreciating and loving our Self deeply, passionately and most importantly, without conditions. It is the realization that we are not who we believe ourselves to be.

Chapter 1

Life

I am not speaking of LIFE as identified in the title, living in full expression. Nor am I asking about the purpose of life, which will be brought to light as you read and contemplate what this book has to offer. Instead, I refer to life as you would define it to someone who might ask, "What is life?" When someone dies at an age that we might consider too young, what do we mean when we say, "His life was cut short"? What do we mean when we say, "Life is not fair"? What do we mean when we say, "Life is precious"? How about the simple statement when something doesn't go according to how we thought it would or should: "That's life." I invite you to take a few minutes to consider how you would answer these questions, not by restating what you have read or what someone else might have said but by considering what actually comes to mind for you. There are no right or wrong answers, only what is true for you at this particular moment.

For me, and for the purpose of this book, life includes the singular and cumulative events and experiences of humanity. Life is each moment, the experience of each moment, as it flows through us. Life is the process of re-gaining clarity of who we are. It is the expression and experience of the Divine through each of us. It is the experience and expression of our own divinity. Life doesn't *happen* to us. Life is created and experienced. Life is our expression of Self. Life is the experience of who we are within the experiences that we create. The act of creation itself is an experience of life. It is through the process of creating and experiencing life that we become aware of, express, and experience fully who we are.

Another way of stating this is that we are both the creator and the creation. As we enjoy and embrace the process of life we create the experiences that ultimately compose our lives. The experiences we create provide the opportunity for our fullest expression and experience of Self.

The Simplexities of Life

Life in and of itself is difficult. It is intended to be so that we can measure and experience the extent of our personal power. However, life is also quite simple. There is nothing distracting it or holding it back. Life doesn't question how or what to do; it just is. It flows whether we are in flow with it or not. It is humanity that brings complexity to life. We try to make it conform to us instead of embracing all life has to offer in the way it is offered. If we were to be fully present to life as it unfolds in each moment we would see a natural, simple process. Life unfolds as it unfolds, not as it should, but as it does, perfectly.

Life will present challenging opportunities that take us to the brink of what we think we are capable of handling. It does so not to break us but to make us whole. It is through the experiences that life presents that we become more aware of whom we are, why we are here and what we are to do.

We say life is unfair because we don't have what we believe we deserve. We feel others have advantages that we have not been given. What we fail to recognize is that life presents exactly what we need in the moment it is needed. Life shows preference to no one. Life is an equal opportunity experience that we choose how to experience.

We judge ourselves against others believing that they are a proper measure of who we are or could be. We struggle to live up to the expectations of others who are likewise struggling to live up to the expectations placed on them instead of respecting the truth of who we are and what we desire. We make conscious decisions that take us away from the experiences we desire to have that result in greater difficulty. We make choices against beliefs we hold without knowing why we believe what we believe, or even if what we believe is true.

We worry about things that have happened and things yet to come. All of which takes us out of the experience of the present moment, the only time there is. It is only in the present moment that we can do anything about anything.

When we are in flow with life, life is simple—not easy but simple. When we resist the flow of life we make it complex and therefore struggle.

Life Is

The appearance is that the world as we now perceive it is out of control. Conflicts, terrorist attacks, shooting rampages, police shootings and corporate and political corruption. Chaos seems to be the flavor of the day with far too many getting a taste.

As I was reflecting on all that I perceive to be happening around the world and the fear that usually results, I took note of where I am sitting and how calm and peaceful it is. Here I am in the midst of peace and quiet yet all around the world events are taking place that are anything but peaceful.

What does it all mean? How did we, humanity, get to this point? Aren't we supposed to be evolving? How are we to cope with all that is happening in the world and live peacefully? How can we cultivate peace when the world appears to be embroiled in chaos? As the questions played out in my mind I became aware of the following stream of consciousness which I simply call, Life is.

Life is difficult. Life is challenging. Life is scary. Life is beautiful. Life is precious. Life is joy. Life is sadness. Life is birth. Life is death. Life is happiness. Life is love. Life is anger. Life is fear. Life is hate. Life is creation. Life is destruction. Life is peace. Life is war. Life is suffering. Life is funny. Life is depressing. Life is pain. Life is healing. Life is compassion. Life is exciting. Life is disappointing. Life is fulfilling. Life is stunning. Life is magnificent. Life is unbelievable. Life is believable. Life is prejudice. Life is acceptance. Life is rejection. Life is simple. Life is complex. Life is spontaneous.

Life is everything we want, everything we don't want, yet everything we need. Life is all that we make it and all that it makes us. Life is the means for revealing and experiencing the truth of who we are. Life matters. You matter. I matter. We all matter. If we didn't matter we wouldn't be here.

What if instead of questioning why this is happening to me, we ask why this is happening for me? Why was I born into the circumstances into which I was born? Why am I having this experience (life)? Why was I born into this family? Why was I born into this race? Why was I born into this religion? Why was I born into this country? Why was I born into this body? Why was I born into these times? What is it that I can and am to gain from the experiences of this lifetime?

This is a difficult world through which to navigate, yet despite it all we have chosen to be here at this place and precise moment in time.

We have done so because it offers exactly what each of us requires to gain the understanding and experience our Soul desires. No one is any better off than another when it comes to the life experiences each is provided. It is only through the comparison and judgment of our own life experiences that this appears to be so.

There is a tendency within humanity to focus on the challenging, difficult and fearful aspects of life when in Truth the energies of peace, joy and love are more pervasive. The media focusing on conflict, terror and tragedy gives the appearance that that is the state of the world. Yes, there are areas and peoples in this world that are and have been in conflict for ages, but that is not reflective of the vast majority of this world and its people. The more attention and energy we put towards the destructive, fearful events of our time the more pervasive they seem and the more impact they have on our lives. This is in essence the theory and intention behind terrorism. Make people believe the world is a terrible frightening place so they live in fear. When we live in fear we subordinate our power to those who perpetuate fear.

"When we live in fear we give away our power to create and live the life we desire, individually and collectively."

Whether we want to admit it or not, we perpetuate the illusion and thereby the experience of fear by the thoughts and beliefs we hold and subsequently share. By writing about, talking about and acting from fear we feed it the power that sustains it.

"What we are in agreement with we bring into the world."

If we truly want to live peaceful lives we must place our focus on those things in life that represent to us peace, love, harmony and beauty. When we focus on these images and feelings we send the energy of them out into the world and then peace, love, harmony and beauty are what we experience in return.This is not about letting those who commit crimes and atrocities do so without consequence. They must be dealt with in an appropriate manner. However, we must change our perspective and belief about life and humanity if we are to change the way life unfolds and is experienced. History repeats itself because no one pays attention. When will we finally understand that all of the events that take place in this world take place because of us, humanity? And that it is us, and only us that can change the way the world will be experienced as we continue on.

When we get to the tipping point of enough people accepting responsibility, individually and collectively, for the events in the world and their personal lives, the change we desire will become our lived experience. And yet, in spite of all of the apparent challenges, injustices and perceived misfortunes of life; despite all of the evidence to the contrary, life is perfect.

Chapter 2

The Purpose of Life

This question has been contemplated since humanity arrived on the Earth plane. It is my belief and understanding that we have chosen to be here to expand our awareness, expression, and experience of who we are. We are not evolving into something more than that which we are, a part of all that is. We are expanding our awareness, knowing, expression and experience of all that is through the experiences of our Self, created specifically for that purpose.

It is often said that the Earth plane is a school in which we are to learn certain lessons. In truth it is a laboratory for experimenting, playing and experiencing the truth of who we are, which has been conveniently forgotten. We are part of all that is, we know all that is; therefore, we have nothing new to learn. There is the appearance of learning or the need to learn; however, it is the experience of the integration of our Divine Spirit and human spirit that is the purpose for our *being* here. This forgetfulness was intentional. If we were fully conscious of who we are, we couldn't have the experiences of life we are here to create. Life's journey is not a mission of Self-discovery; it is a mission of Self-recovery.

It's funny if you think about it. One of the crimes with which society is most concerned at this time is identity theft—stealing your identity for the purpose of gaining access to your assets and using them for personal gain and benefit. While identity theft in the way we experience it in today's society is a serious crime and is most certainly a real threat, each of us is the greatest perpetrator of identity theft that can be imagined. We have stolen our own identity by denying our True Self. We live in Self-denial. Not only do we live in Self-denial but we create a new false identity that appears to be true because it is who we believe our Self to be. We even fight to protect and sustain it out of fear that someone else might steal it.

As we remember who we are through our experiences we become aware of the influence we have on our own lives and the lives of others. We gain an awareness of the influence of our thoughts, words, and actions on how life unfolds. We take responsibility for our life and realize that our response to life is what creates the experiences that allow us to expand our knowing (remembrance) of who we are.

What we do in life, our career or vocation, is only a vehicle for expressing who we are, however it does not define us. We define (express and experience) who we are through who we are being in the role(s) we have chosen. As an example, do you want to be remembered as a successful attorney, teacher, artist, or real estate agent? Or do you want to be remembered as someone who embraced, appreciated, and lived life to the fullest and in so doing served as an example to others of what life can be? Regardless of the role you choose it will always offer the opportunity to express and experience your Self as an aspect of the Divine.

We fully express who we are through our relationships with and to all things, including our Self. Through our expression we demonstrate our level of passion for life. It is from within our passion for life that our life's passions are revealed. We are to know the Universe desires us to be happy, healthy, and well. We are to acknowledge, allow, accept and enjoy all that life has to offer.

Being passionate about life is honoring, respecting, and embracing the journey we are on. It is living from the knowledge that we have and are creating our life journey. Being passionate about life is the knowing that within each moment lays the potential to expand our experience and expression of our Self. It is also honoring and respecting the journey of others because we know it is of their choosing. Being passionate about life is being open to and allowing the experience of our magnificence.

Life's Purpose

What an incredible time of year. As I write trees are ablaze with vibrant reds, golds, and oranges and stand in silhouette against the tangerine and blue early morning sky. The air is crisp, clear, and clean. There is an energy that flows through everything in preparation for the long winter slumber. There is a beauty that this time of year offers that is like no other as Mother Nature makes yet another seasonal transition.

Like Nature we experience seasons during the course of our lifetime(s). We have periods of time when we are immersed in a particular experience until we transition to the next. We can experience a season of extreme joy and happiness that transitions to a season of ill health and difficulty that transitions to a season of recovery and renewed joy. We can be in a season of a difficult relationship and transition to a season of solitude and peace. Whatever the season, allow your Self to see the perfection and beauty in it. Embrace it, feel it, and most importantly, enjoy it. Open your Self to receiving and experiencing the grandeur in each unfolding season. Each season allows for an experience and expression of our Self that a previous season could not.

Just as Nature expresses herself in all of her glory, we are here to express and experience our Self in all of our glory. Our purpose is to enjoy the process of LIFE fully, completely and wholly (holy) as we experience and express our Self, fully, completely and wholly (holy).

There is a difference between the purpose of life and one's life purpose, although they sound very similar. The purpose of life, our existence in human form, is for the fullest experience and expression of the Divine through us in our fullest experience and expression of Self. Our life's purpose is to express and experience the Divine through our Self-expression, in whatever form of expression we choose, as we remember the truth of who we are.

"Humanity is one of the vehicles through which the Divine is experienced and expressed."

As I journey through my life coaching individuals and speaking with different groups of people, invariably I am asked questions about life's purpose. Here are a few of the most frequently asked along with my response:

1. *Do I have a life purpose?* The answer is quite simple: yes, otherwise you wouldn't be here. Our overall life purpose is the expression of the Divine through our experience and expression of Self in as wide a range of experiences as possible. This is done through the many different personalities we take on in many different lifetimes. As we fully experience and express Self, the Divine is fully expressed.

   Additionally, as each of us is in the process of experiencing and expressing our Self we play roles in the lives of those around us so they too can experience and express their Self as fully and completely as possible.

2. *How do I know if I am fulfilling my life's purpose?* Again, the answer is simple. You are fulfilling your life's purpose because you are here. There is no right or wrong way to do so. Every experience we have in each lifetime, including those we might label as wrong or bad, is another experience and expression of Self. Our purpose is to have the widest range of experiences of Self as possible as we remember who we truly are.

3. *Is who I am or what I do relevant?* Am I relevant? Is what I bring to those around me relevant? When I am asked this question, I respond with another question: "Relevant in relation to what?" Most often, this comes down to whether or not one believes their life has meaning and benefits others. Do I make a difference? What does the world gain by my presence? These questions take us back to the real issue of the value we place upon our Self, the love we have for our Self and the trust we have in our Self versus the opinions, values and expectations we accept about our Self placed upon us by others.

   Relevancy is a judgment of whether or not we are good enough or have something to offer. This deep-seated judgment is not that of other people but of our own beliefs about our Self. Does it really matter if others believe you are good enough or relevant? It only matters if you allow it to matter. It only matters if you base your value of Self on what others might say or think about you. Your opinion of your Self is all that matters and is the only thing that is relevant.

   Now you might say that if you have an opinion of your Self

as unworthy and another person whom you respect has an opinion of you as very worthy and relevant, then that other person's opinion matters. Well, in a way it matters in that it offers you a different perspective. However, until you change your opinion of your Self the opinion of the other makes no difference and therefore does not matter. What matters is your opinion of your Self, an opinion that only you can change at any time in any given moment.

4. *Are we relevant?* Absolutely, we would not be here if we were not. Another way to look at our relevancy is from the perspective of whether or not the world is relevant without us.

"Some might question our relevancy in this world. I question the relevancy of this world without us."

We are each unique in the experience and expression of our Self during each lifetime. We are here to participate and support one another throughout the process of Self-recovery. No life is irrelevant regardless of its length or how it was played out. Each Soul is here to experience and express its Self fully and completely within the context of all that each lifetime offers.

5. *Do I make a difference? If so, how?* A basic desire that we all share as humans is wanting to make a difference in the world and in the lives of others. I want to assure you first and foremost that you are making a difference, otherwise you wouldn't be here. Yes, some will say that is too easy an answer. Where is the proof?

The truth is that most of us won't change the world through a monumental act, discovery, invention or extraordinary life. And yet, who we are and what we do has the same effect and impact on those with whom we connect as those we hold in high regard like Martin Luther King, Albert Einstein, Mother Teresa or even Pablo Picasso. Those who we consider world changers didn't fully comprehend the impact they would have by being who they were and what they did. They did what they did because of who they were and thereby made a difference in the world.

"Being true to oneself, and living in full expression of that truth, is all that it takes to make a difference in this world."

We have a far greater impact on this world and the lives of others than we could possibly imagine. We might not be consciously aware of the difference because most often it will happen through what appear to be random, disconnected events that somehow come together to reach and benefit those for whom it was intended.

"Live in full expression of who you truly are and the world benefits from the gift of your expression."

When world events take place like natural disasters, war or terrorist attacks and you experience feelings of hopelessness or helplessness, know without doubt that even though you might not be able to impact those directly affected by the events, that you are making a difference. You do this by being who you are, wherever you are and your heart-felt compassion for those directly affected. If you were meant to be somewhere else, you would be. If you were meant to be other than who you are, you would be. We are always in the perfect place to impact the world and others in the way that we are intended to impact them.

Chapter 3

Cycle of L.I.F.E.

We are not here to evolve; we are here to experience and express who we are, always have been and always will be. What is expanding is our knowledge or remembrance of Self and therefore, our experience and expression of Self. The more aware we become of who we are and always have been, the grander our experience and expression of Self. It is within this expansion process that we move through four phases of experience and expression during each lifetime on the Earth plane.

The four phases of the life cycle are reflection, revelation, reconciliation, and resurrection. We can experience all four phases several times in a single lifetime or we can experience them once in a single lifetime. We can also experience all four as they are spread out over the course of several lifetimes. How quickly we move through the phases is dependent upon the experiences and expression of Self that our Soul desires and chooses to have during each incarnation.

Once you read the description of each phase you might question how we can move through all four phases multiple times in one lifetime if the final phase is resurrection. It would seem that after resurrection a Soul's journey is complete and it ascends. What you will discover is that each cycle expands upon the previous cycle with each cycle resulting in a grander experience and expression of Self than the one previous.

The Four Phases

Reflection is the questioning phase. We question why things are the way they are, why we are the way we are, or why things happen the way they do. We question the purpose and meaning of events in our personal lives as well as events around the world. We question our beliefs about life and more specifically, about our Self.

In this phase we notice the limiting beliefs we hold that have prevented us from living in full experience and expression of Self. We question our relevance and purpose. It is also the phase in which we consider how we individually and collectively fit into the Divine design and perfection of all things.

Reflection causes us to consider where we are in life in comparison to where we thought we would be at a particular moment. Reflection is not about right or wrong; good or bad. It is the acknowledgment of what has been and what is to this moment. We consider our life experiences without judgment and recognize they are just that, life experiences. Reflection is the key that opens the door to revelation, the phase of LIFE in which we recognize life doesn't have to continue in the way it has up to this moment; there is always a choice.

Revelation is the phase in which we begin to experience more of who we are. We gain a deeper understanding and meaning of the purpose of life. Even though we gain awareness during the phase of reflection, it is in the phase of revelation that our awareness becomes more expansive. We become more aware of whom we are in relation to life and all of creation. We begin to gain an understanding of the power within us to consciously create our life experiences as we desire them to be. We begin to take responsibility for our life experiences by becoming consciously aware of the correlation between our thoughts, beliefs, and feelings, and how our life unfolds. We begin to see and accept our connection to the Divine and All That Is.

Reconciliation is the phase in which we accept our expanded knowledge and experience of who we know ourselves to be. Our awareness continues to expand and therefore our knowledge and acceptance of who we are continues to expand. We gain a greater understanding of our place in the Universe and our purpose for living in human form on the Earth plane.

We have begun to more consciously experience and express the integration of our Spiritual aspect with our Human aspect. Even though these two aspects of Self have always been present within us, reconciliation is the activation of these two aspects of Self functioning as one. We accept the truth of how powerful we are, of whom we are and we create new, more desired life experiences from this knowing. We consciously exercise the power of choice.

Resurrection is our rising up from the metaphorical death of our previous expression of Self that we experience as we move through this four-phase process. The resurrected or enhanced expression and experience of Self in our lived reality is a result of the expanded knowledge and awareness gained through the experiences of the other three phases.

Resurrection is the integration phase in which we more fully experience and express our Divinity as we have come to know it in that moment. We come back to LIFE. We consciously live in full expression and experience of who we are in that and every moment. We trust and live from the knowledge of who we are. We trust Life in all of its expressions knowing its intention is our greater experience and expression of Self. We resurrect our experience and expression of Self from the illusion of who we thought we were to the experience of who we now know our Self to be; our True Self.

As we move through each phase we do so seamlessly. There is no line of demarcation that tells us we have moved from one to another. More often than not, it is after we move through a cycle that we become aware of a greater sense of Self. This usually occurs when we are back in the reflection phase and are taking note of who we are and where we are along our life's path. No one phase is more important than another as each is integral to the cycle of LIFE (living in full expression).

As we move through these four phases and gain a greater understanding of our True Self we do so through the context of what I refer to as the four pillars of life. They are the underpinning of our full expression of the Truth of who we are.

Chapter 4

The Four Pillars of L.I.F.E.

The four pillars of L.I.F.E. we are here to express, experience and embody during our lifetime(s) are non-judgment, unconditional love, gratitude and forgiveness. They are not listed in any particular order because they are equally important and integral to each other. As an example, unconditional love cannot be experienced or expressed if we are not forgiving or non-judgmental. And gratitude in and of itself is love being expressed unconditionally for all that we have, all that is available to us, and all that we are.

As life unfolds we are presented opportunities to experience and express our Self through the embodiment of these four pillars. We embody them for our personal experience of them and as an outward expression for and toward others. Those throughout history whom we consider our most influential spiritual leaders did so as well. They were not (are not) here to teach us what to do but rather to exemplify through their embodiment and full expression who we are and what we are capable of creating and experiencing. At our core we are non-judgment, forgiveness, unconditional love and gratitude.

First and foremost, these four pillars are to be experienced by and expressed towards our Self. Our experience of the outside world is a reflection of our inner experience and relationship with our Self. Therefore, we cannot fully express and experience what we do not embody.

"We cannot be the full expression of that which we are not."

Some believe this to be an act of selfishness. After all we have been taught to give and be supportive of all others, in many cases without regard to our own feelings or needs. The term used for giving oneself fully and completely in this way is being "selfless". However, when we give to others without regard to our own feelings and desires being met, being selfless, we are less of our true Self. This isn't to imply we shouldn't be supportive, kind, loving or concerned with the well-being of others, on the contrary. The more loving, forgiving, grateful and non-judgmental we are towards our Self, the greater our capacity and desire to be this way towards others.

As we are the embodiment of these four pillars—non-judgment, unconditional love, forgiveness and gratitude—we enjoy the grandest experience, expression and relationship with our Self. Simultaneously we serve as an example to others how they too can enjoy the grandest experience, expression and relationship with their Self.

Non-Judgment

Of the four pillars we are here to experience and express during our lifetime(s) I find non-judgment to be the most difficult and opportunistic. We judge things, ourselves and other people against one another, someone else, or something else. In so doing we label them as better or worse, good or evil, ugly or beautiful, worthy or unworthy, right or wrong. Why is it so difficult to let go of judgment and accept and embrace life as it is, as it unfolds in perfection?

What is judgment? Quite simply it is a person's opinion based on their perspective. Their perspective was formed from information and beliefs they hold as true, regardless of the truth of the information or belief.

Another important consideration when it comes to judgment is that we do not know what another person has gone through or is currently going through. We see the outward manifestation of who they are in the moment and judge them against what we believe that manifestation or behavior would indicate. We do not and cannot know the journey another Soul has chosen any more than they can know ours. Quite frankly, it is not ours to know or understand. However, it is ours to honor and respect. It is the same consideration we would ask as we explore, express and experience our Self in the way we have chosen on this souljourn.

The real issue of judgment is Self- judgment. To judge someone or something says who we are and where we are in our experience and expression of our Self. It has nothing to do with the person or thing being judged. Judgment at its core is a reflection of one's beliefs about, and relationship with, their Self.

Take notice of how you judge yourself and how often you judge yourself. Not the outward expression of self-judgment, although this does happen, but more so the internal judgment of Self through the consistent self-talk or inner dialogue you continue to have with your Self.

What do you continuously say to and about your Self through thoughts and words that reinforce specific behaviors and beliefs you hold about your Self that are limiting and disempowering? Do you speak or think of yourself in Self-deprecating ways? Are you holding yourself back from the full expression and experience of the Self you desire because of your judgment of who you think you are or need to be?

Conversely, how often do you speak highly of your Self? How often are your thoughts kind, loving, empowering and inspirational? How often, if ever, do you say to your Self from the heart, "I love you, I appreciate you, I honor and respect you"?

The point is that we must first be non-judgmental towards our Self if we are to be non-judgmental towards all others. In truth we cannot be non-judgmental until we are non-judgmental towards our Self. When we are accepting, appreciative, respectful and loving towards our Self we are accepting, appreciative and loving towards all others. When we acknowledge, accept and honor the path we have chosen for the fullest expression and experience of Self, we can then fully honor the path that each other Soul has chosen for their desired expression and experience of Self.

Whenever I find myself being judgmental, whether about my Self or another, I ask very simple, yet revealing questions. What is it in me that this is so? What is it I believe about myself in this moment that is causing me to form this opinion or judgment? What is it that I can look at about myself that is being shown to me through my judgment? From where did these beliefs originate? And perhaps most importantly, are they true?

Any beliefs (judgments) we hold about ourselves that are disempowering or that would not allow or support the full expression and experience of our Self are not the truth of who we truly are, who we desire to be or who we are in the process of being.

Being judgmental doesn't make us right or wrong. That thought is in and of itself judgmental. It is simply who and where we believe our Self to be in that moment of our current life experience and expression of Self. It is through the recognition of our judgment that we can change our beliefs and therefore our expression and experience of Self.

Being non-judgmental doesn't mean we accept or condone what someone else is doing or has done. It doesn't mean we turn a blind eye to things that are or could be harmful to others. On the contrary, we do what we can to prevent or alter the event or circumstances without judgment of the person or people. This is difficult at times. However, it is when we rise above our judgmental tendencies that we are in greater alignment with our Divine nature. The more aligned we are with our Divine nature the greater our experience and expression of our Self.

Imagine how different the world would be if we didn't judge ourselves and therefore one another. What if each of us allowed each other to be who we are and desire to be? There would be no war, no prejudice, no discrimination, no hatred, no religious intolerance, no poverty, no hunger, just peace and collaboration.

Out of non-judgment comes unconditional love. With unconditional love we are accepting of all others and all things as they exist in their perfection. There would be differences in how we think and live and certainly some differences in what each believes. Yet, there would be respect for one another and an honoring of the life path that each has chosen for their personal expression and experience of Self. There would be the full responsibility for one's life experiences while accepting and allowing others to be responsible for theirs.

Practicing non-judgment can be difficult. To lessen or eliminate the degree to which you judge I suggest two things. First, when you find yourself being judgmental of another simply send them love, respect and blessings for their chosen journey. Express gratitude for their expression that has brought to your attention your judgment. Be grateful and appreciative towards your Self for the awareness of your judgment and willingness to change.

Secondly, bring your awareness to bear on your judgments. Question your judgments and the beliefs behind them. Ask, what is it in me that this is so? As you acknowledge your judgment and reveal the underlying belief you will alter your relationship with your Self. As you alter your relationship with Self your judgmental tendencies dissipate. As they dissipate you gain a greater acceptance, appreciation, respect and love for your Self and all others. As you gain greater acceptance, appreciation, respect and love for all others you are living from the heart within which resides unconditional love.

Unconditional Love

Unconditional love is a state of being. It is our purest form of being. It is our fullest expression and experience of Self. It is in this state that we are authentic, "not far removed from source, of undisputed origin." Unconditional love is love in its purest, most simple form and expression. It is love as love is, always has been and always will be.

Before I get too deep into the discussion of unconditional love I have a confession to make. It is time to dispel the myth of unconditional love. It might be difficult for some to understand and accept, however, I believe if you honestly think about it you will come to the same conclusion. Unconditional love does not exist. Anything that we would consider love that is attached to or conditioned upon something that is outside of love itself is not love at all. Love predicated on acting or being a certain way or in conforming to what is believed to be worthy of love is not love.

You might ask why unconditional love is included as one of the four pillars of LIFE if it does not exist. It is included because we experience *human love* as a romantic form of love with its attendant feelings and emotions. We also have a belief of what constitutes unconditional love because we have been told that unconditional love is love in its purest form. We have been told that GOD's love for us is unconditional. We say our love for our children is unconditional. However, the very fact that we could contemplate the possibility of unconditional love means there is a belief in the possibility of love with conditions.

Conditional love says "I will love you but only if you act a certain way, if you believe in certain things or do certain things for me." Love is our deepest, most heart-felt expression. It is our fullest expression and experience of our Self and therefore the Divine. Love is as love is. Any love that we accept upon which there are conditions is a reflection of the conditions we have placed upon our love for our Self. The love that is included in the four pillars of life is Divine love. Our purpose for being on this planet is to live in full expression of the truth of who we are. That truth is Divine Love.

When we are fully accepting and loving of our Self, when we embody Divine Love, that love is reflected in the outer world. To embody Divine Love, to be the living experience and expression of Divine Love in human form requires we do nothing more than consciously experience and express that which we are. In doing so we are free of any thoughts, beliefs or judgments about our Self that would prevent the fullest experience and expression of Divine Love possible.

Final Thought on Unconditional Love

What I know...the quality of life, my life, is not determined by what GOD might shine upon me but on what I shine upon myself. GOD's love is constant, ever present and without condition. To believe that I have to be or act a certain way to be worthy of GOD's love or anyone's love is my ego telling me that I am not good enough or deserving of love as I am. To withhold love from me or anyone until I act or believe in a certain way is judgment. Divine Love, GOD, is non-judgmental.

The world returns to me what I believe about my Self. My experiences of Life are a reflection of my inner sight, my relationship with and belief in Self. As I see and believe in my Self, as I love my Self, the world returns to me those life experiences. It is in honoring, appreciating, nurturing, commending and loving my Self without conditions that the world responds in kind. It is in loving my Self fully and completely that I offer humanity the greatest gift I have to offer, the expression of Divine Love.

Gratitude

Gratitude is attentive appreciation towards all that we are, all that we have, all that we experience, and the potential for all that can be. It is an expression and experience of Divine Love for all that we are, all that we have, all that we experience, and the potential for all that can be.

There is a law of gratitude just as there is a law of gravity. We can't see gravity but we know it exists. We know to a certain degree what gravity is and that it is at work whether we are consciously aware of it or not. We don't have to think about gravity to know that it keeps planets in alignment, us on the face of the Earth and that it causes the ebb and flow of the tides. Thinking about gravity doesn't make it any more so, gravity just is.

Gratitude on the other hand has one very important distinction. The more we are aware and conscious of it, the more we express it, the more we are given for which to be grateful. The more we demonstrate that we appreciate all that we have and all that is available to us, the more the Universe responds by giving us more.

So just how does this law of gratitude work? When we demonstrate gratitude, heartfelt gratitude, through our thoughts, words and deeds we emit an energetic frequency of love, joy, peace and thankfulness. As this energetic frequency is emitted it attracts like energetic frequencies that present similar experiences for the feeling and expression of gratitude.

The Universe wants us to experience love, joy, happiness and well-being. Therefore, it will co-create with us those experiences that allow for these feelings to be experienced and expressed. All that we desire lies in wait as the potential for it to be. We bring it into our lived experience with our attentive appreciation that it is ours should we choose to receive it.

Being in a state of gratitude we are open and receptive to what the Universe wants us to experience, in fact, what the Universe has promised as our birthright. In gratitude we live life with an understanding and acceptance that there is an abundance of everything we desire readily available to everyone at all times. Not just a select few.

Living with this abundance mentality dissolves all thoughts of lack or limit to which we might become attached. In being released from these limiting thoughts and beliefs we make room for that which we truly desire. By expressing gratitude, we are empowered and no longer question our worthiness to receive the goodness of life. In gratitude, we receive and experience all that we desire.

Keys to the Law of Gratitude

Gratitude must be heart-felt and sincere. It must arise from the truth of who we know our Self to be. It is expressed without ego based intentions that we will receive something in return.

Gratitude is expressed in thought, word and deed. What we say, think and do is an expression of gratitude for all that we are, all that we have, and all that we experience.

Gratitude is expressed for anything and everything for which we have been blessed, which in Truth is everything we have been given and everything we have available to us. It is expressed without any judgment or thought about that which we *think* we do not have.

When gratitude is expressed we are asking that for which we are expressing gratitude, also be given to all others.

Forgiveness

Of the four pillars of LIFE forgiveness is the most liberating. It is also the one I am having the most difficulty writing about. It isn't because I don't know how to forgive or that I have not forgiven. I have long since been able to detach the person from the event and accept that they are not what they do or have done. It stems more from my difficulty in forgiving myself, as well as letting go of any doubts, fears or judgments I have regarding my Self.

So what is this act of forgiveness? Forgiveness is releasing oneself from thoughts, beliefs and judgments held against oneself or another. It is one of the greatest expressions of Self-love we can have. When we forgive we tear down the walls of a Self-imposed prison built upon a foundation of anger, resentment, judgment, hatred and fear.

Forgiveness is one of the greatest expressions of compassion we can extend to our Self and others. We extend compassion for our humanness and the respective path each Soul has chosen to experience and express what the Soul desires. Forgiveness does not suggest we become friends with, or even like, those whom we feel have harmed us. Yet through forgiveness we acknowledge that we do not know what pain caused them to act in the way they did any more than they can know ours.

I want to add another perspective regarding forgiveness for your consideration. For many this will seem unbelievable but I ask for your consideration anyway. This is the idea that the experience(s) involving you and another was agreed upon by each Soul prior to this incarnation. In fact, it could have been agreed upon by many Souls who were to participate in the experience, it really doesn't matter. What matters is that what took place was intentional. It was done for the benefit of one or all involved in the event.

Your forgiveness might just be your recognition of these other brave Souls who played out the role to which they agreed so that you could enjoy this experience and expression of your Self within the context of the event. And it could also be that you agreed to be the so called victim so the other(s) could experience their Self in the role to which they agreed.

Forgiveness holds within it non-judgment, love and gratitude for all that life has to offer. Forgiveness allows us to more fully experience and express our true nature. Forgiveness allows us to be detached from thoughts and beliefs that would hold us hostage and prevent our grandest experience and expression of Self. Forgiveness offers the opportunity to liberate and be liberated.

Forgiveness is not about condoning or absolving someone of something they did. It is not turning a blind eye and acting as if the event never took place. What was done was done, forgiveness will not change that. In forgiveness the offender is not being released from the act committed. They might feel better thinking that because they have been forgiven all is well. Forgiveness doesn't alter the fact that the offender must live with what they have done in addition to coping with the consequences of their act. True forgiveness comes from taking responsibility and forgiving one's Self for the actions that were taken. Only in Self -forgiveness is one truly free.

The paradox in forgiveness is that the very act that causes us to harbor anger, resentment, hatred or contempt for another is the catalyst for a grander expression and experience of our Self. The act of forgiveness provides the opportunity to rise above that which would hold us back.

Another seeming paradox of the act of forgiveness is that although we are seeking to be released from the feelings we hold; we are also to fully experience them. We are to be angry, resentful and perhaps feel contempt for the other person. We are here to experience and express the full range of human emotions as an experience and expression of Self.

In addition, we are to release the energy behind these emotions so they don't become blocks within us that would prevent life from continuing to flow through us.

Most of what has been shared regarding forgiveness has been about extending forgiveness towards another in an effort to be released from the disempowering thoughts and beliefs attached to the event and/or the person or people involved. It is easy to believe that forgiveness is about the other person. When in Truth forgiveness is always about us. It is our thoughts and beliefs that keep anger, hatred, frustration, resentment and contempt alive in our own heart; not the other person. As we forgive and release our Self from these feelings and emotions we live more in the moment, and are more fully engaged and available to what life is offering.

*"Forgiveness is the conscious choice to be free.
In forgiveness lies the Truth,
In Truth we are set free."*

When forgiveness is expressed, the one for whom forgiveness is given takes responsibility for their act, while the one who is forgiving takes responsibility for their own peace and happiness.

"In Truth there is nothing to forgive."

Chapter 5

The Power of Belief

This might seem to be a strange question, however, it is one of the most powerful questions we can answer. Do you believe? Do I believe what? You might ask. Do you believe you have the power within you to be who you desire to be and to experience what you desire to experience? Do you believe you have the power within you to make changes in your life that would allow for the fullest experience and expression of Self possible?

Underlying all of our actions and subsequent experiences are our beliefs about whether or not we can do what we desire to do or be. It is our belief in our Self that determines the degree to which we experience life as we desire. Awareness and the desire for change are the initial steps in shattering the illusions of limiting beliefs; however, we could easily say it is a belief that change is possible that fuels the desire to create it.

It was brought to my attention many years ago that what we believe is the result of what we have read, what others have told us, or what we have observed. Very little of what we believe actually comes from personal experience. And even when we do observe something firsthand it is being filtered through the beliefs we already hold that may or may not be true. What does this say about the quality of our decisions and the resulting experiences? How far from the Truth might we be as a result of decisions we have made and continue to make based on these beliefs? Does this mean we were or are wrong? No, it just means that what we believe is what we accept and consent to as true up to this moment.

"Our life experiences become that to which we consent and accept as true."

Several years ago I took a look at my beliefs and how I had come to accept them. Throughout this process I examined my beliefs about everything in my life, including politics, religion, society, relationships, spirituality, and family. But nowhere were my beliefs more critical than those I held about my Self. I looked at decisions that resulted in less than favorable outcomes, or that prevented me from experiences that would have brought me greater joy, greater happiness and success. I questioned my underlying beliefs about myself and life that led to my making those decisions. This wasn't an exercise to prove myself or others wrong, or to cause undue stress or discomfort. It was for gaining clarity. The more we understand why we believe what we believe, the more truthful our beliefs. The more truthful our beliefs, the better our decisions and the more consciously we create our life experiences.

The greater our understanding of who we know our Self to be and of what we are capable of creating and experiencing, the easier it is to shatter the illusion of the limiting beliefs we hold. A simple exercise for examining one's beliefs that is both mentally and spiritually freeing is to answer these two questions:

1. Are the beliefs that I hold mine?
2. Are the beliefs that I hold true?

As you answer these questions you will discover that there are many beliefs you hold about your Self and life that are not true and were not yours to begin with. This is an important step in the process of being released from limiting beliefs. When you acknowledge that what you hold as true is nothing more than what you have consented to and accepted as true, you regain your personal power. With empowerment you accept responsibility for your life and therefore can effect the change you desire. You come to realize you do not have to accept who you *think* you are, where you are, or what you are doing. You are not stuck in a pre-programmed life with no input or impact on what happens to or around you.

In fact, just the opposite is true. You are an actor in humanity's play. You are simultaneously the writer, actor, and director. This means that at any moment you do not like what is playing out in your life you can write and act out a new script based on your innermost wants, desires and inspirations.

"You are the creator and the creation."

The ability to create these new life experiences comes through the gift of imagination. All creation begins in thought. It is imagination that provides the freedom to create a virtual reality of what it is you want to be and experience. When your lived experiences begin to reflect this virtual reality, you become aware of the immense creative power of your thoughts. The more consciously aware you are of this power, the more empowered you become. The more empowered you become, the more consciously you create your life experiences.

Shattering the Illusions

Have you ever had the experience of really wanting to do something but for some reason, mostly unknown, you convinced yourself to do otherwise? You had a strong desire to move in a direction that was new and exciting but held back. It held the potential for an amazing new life experience; perhaps even open you to new areas of possibility. And what happened? From somewhere within thoughts bubbled into your consciousness that convinced you that you were not good enough, creative enough, worthy enough, or talented enough to have this new and exciting experience. You told yourself this new experience was for people who were more deserving, more talented and more skilled than you. As a result, you didn't follow through.

"What if instead of getting lost in self-doubt, we get lost in our magnificence?"

Have you ever considered why we are given the inspirations we are given? Are they some cruel joke played on us by an unsympathetic Universe to get us excited only to let us down? Or could they be intentions of the Soul that we are to experience in this lifetime?

How do we change the thoughts and beliefs that limit our expressing and experiencing all that we are and can be? How do we move beyond these beliefs that are subconsciously held so we can create and live the life of our desires? How do we recognize and accept that limiting beliefs are nothing more than illusions *we* have created?

"Our limiting beliefs are the invisible chains that bind us."

My experience of writing this book loosened those invisible chains that bind me. However, there are still limiting beliefs that surface that would hold me back if I allowed them. The key here is *if I allow them.* They only exist because I allow them to exist. The only things preventing my fullest experience and expression of Self are the beliefs I hold about what is holding me back. These are the things that follow, "I can't do this because__________." Or, "If I do this, then __________."

Why do we create these illusions? What is it in each one of us that would cause us to hold onto limiting thoughts and beliefs that deny us the grandest experience and expression of Self and therefore the life we truly desire? Where do these limiting beliefs come from? Why do we defend them and make decisions based on them, especially decisions that limit what we are so capable of doing?

A lot of time could be spent trying to figure out why we have these beliefs, but it doesn't really matter. Knowing (believing) a belief might have come from the way we were brought up doesn't change the fact that we hold the belief and are allowing it to limit the way we experience and express our Self now. However, knowing that we hold a particular belief does present the opportunity to release it. In assuming responsibility, we consciously take steps to move beyond the beliefs thereby breaking down the walls of our self-imposed prison.

This doesn't mean taking responsibility for the event or circumstances that created the belief. Only that we take responsibility for the fact that we continue to hold onto it. It is then and only then that we have the power to create change, for in truth we can only change what we create.

"When we become aware of and acknowledge our limiting beliefs we are able to transcend them."

A powerful way I have discovered for freeing myself from any limiting beliefs is to recognize and accept that everything that has happened in my life is nothing more than an experience of my life. What happened doesn't define me and it certainly can't determine what will happen from this moment forward unless I give it the power to do so. It was an experience and expression of my Self in the moment the event took place. Just as every experience from this moment forward will be an experience and expression of my Self in that moment. The big *aha* was the awareness of my role as co-creator of these experiences that allow for my full experience and expression of Self.

> *"What happened doesn't matter.*
> *What matters is what happens."*

One More Thing

There is another aspect of limiting beliefs that is important and vital to living in full expression—not from the standpoint of where existing limiting beliefs might have originated, but where new limiting beliefs can originate. We typically concern ourselves with our personal limiting beliefs without taking into consideration the influence of the limiting beliefs of others. How often do we deny ourselves new experiences or opportunities because someone else says it is not possible or that we don't have the right skills or experience to do it?

We might be told that something is too challenging or difficult or will take too much time. All too often we become overly concerned with what others might think or say and as a result decide not to move forward on something for which we were previously deeply inspired. The truth is what someone else says has nothing to do with you. It is who and where they are at that moment in time that dictates how they feel, what they say and what they believe is possible.

For example, say you tell a family member something you are considering and that person's response is to tell you that you don't have the necessary skills, qualifications or knowledge. Now, because of those comments you decide not to move forward. Not only have you taken ownership of that person's limiting belief, but you have now made that person's opinion of what is possible for you more important than your own inner knowing.

People's thoughts and opinions are based on what they believe is possible for them, but they take on the appearance of what we can or cannot do when directed towards us. Most often, it is not done intentionally. Somewhere within them is a limiting belief they are not good enough, smart enough, or brave enough to take on the task or opportunity. Sometimes, especially with family members, it is done because in their mind they are trying to protect us. They tell us that something can't be done or that we shouldn't attempt it in an effort to help us avoid hurt or disappointment.

Unfortunately, it is also done out of the fear that we might accomplish or experience something much grander than what they have experienced. They de-value themselves with these beliefs because they are measuring themselves against what we do instead of recognizing that anyone's true value or worth is in who they are regardless of what is accomplished.

This was my experience in writing this book. I was told I had no credibility, no expertise or qualification in the subject matter. I was asked why anyone would pay to hear what I have to say. I was even asked why I thought I was chosen? If I had listened to this so-called advice you wouldn't be reading this material. Perhaps more importantly, I wouldn't be living in full expression of who I am and would not have the experience of my Self gained through the writing of this book.

I learned through this process and experience that credibility is not gained through the approval of other people, but rather through the truthful expression of who one is. No one outside of you can give you credibility. Nor can anyone outside of you take it away. One's worth is who they are, not what they do, what they have or what they experience.

Just as important as our awareness of the influence of others' limiting beliefs on us is the awareness of the influence of our limiting beliefs on others. When you catch yourself telling someone they shouldn't do something or that it is not possible, question why you feel that way. Ask yourself, "What is it in me that this is so?" Understand that when you tell someone that something is not possible for them there is something within you preventing your full expression.

Here are some key thoughts to consider that will help you rise above and move beyond limiting beliefs:

- Our beliefs are thoughts we hold as true however they might not be the truth. It is only what we believe to be true based on the information we have to that moment.
- Our thoughts, like everything else, are energy. By releasing the limiting belief, we release the energy of that belief and are therefore released from the power it holds over us.
- Have faith and trust in the process of life. Trust in the goodness of life knowing that your happiness, health, and wellbeing are what is intended for you and that what is intended is always provided.
- Know that you are always more than good enough. You are worthy of and deserve whatever goodness shows up in your life; otherwise it would not have shown up.
- Know that whatever life presents is always in your highest and best good regardless of its appearance; otherwise it would never have been presented.

- Know that when something is presented that is considered challenging or difficult, it is for your personal and spiritual growth and expansion. It is not presented to test you; it offers you the opportunity to more fully experience and express your Self within the context of that specific life event. All that is necessary for your expansion, expression, and experience of Self is always presented.
- You are and have always been loved; you are and have always been appreciated beyond measure, and you have never been and never will be alone.

Nature's Demonstration

When writing on uncertainty a few years ago, I ran into a little writer's block and felt the need to take a break. I find that getting outside in nature allows my mind to clear. While outside I decided to do a little yard work, in particular, some weeding in front of my house. As I was pulling out the unwanted plants their roots seemed to go on forever. I was amazed by how far and deep the roots had grown. As I pulled the plants the stems would snap allowing me to only remove the upper part of the plant. It became apparent that if I didn't completely remove the roots the unwanted plants would grow back.

Then it dawned on me, Nature (the Universe) was presenting the perfect illustration of what needs to be done with our deeply rooted and held beliefs. We can work on the surface issues and bring about temporary results and enjoy some success. However, it is not until we do the work beneath the surface that the root cause is removed and we create the richer, fuller, more rewarding life experiences we desire.

"When we rise above our core limiting beliefs the miraculous and its potential lies before us."

What we need to understand and accept is that the Universe is biased toward life. Regardless of the harshest of conditions life will somehow find a way to flourish. Examples in nature are trees and plants growing out of solid rock without any apparent soil or means of nourishment. Another example is plants that flourish in the desert where it appears that life of any kind could not survive.

The same holds true for us. The Universe is biased toward our life, our fulfillment of what we desire to express and experience. All we have to do is show is our willingness to trust the process. This is done by stepping into the uncertainty of life and letting go of any fears and beliefs that would convince us there is nothing we can do even when we find ourselves under challenging or harsh circumstances.

Although I use the term "step into the uncertainty of life," life is not uncertain. Life is definitive in its perfect unfoldment and expression. Life always provides what is needed when it is needed. It is our perception of life that creates uncertainty. If we do not trust the process of life and therefore fear, we will not receive what we most desire and believe we need. We have become comfortable in the certainty of our discomfort even though we would like things to be better. Instead of stepping into the vastness of the Universe (our magnificence) we remain small in a limiting self-created world.

What I have come to accept as truth is that the Universe rewards courage and expansion. The more courageous we are in stepping into our magnificence, stepping into the full expression and experience of who we are, the more the Universe conspires to make it so. The more we expand our experience of Self by stepping into our magnificence, the more courageous we become. Life will not and cannot let us down. Life always (all ways) provides what is needed when it is needed, whether it is accepted or not. The choice is always ours. How do you choose?

Chapter 6

The Life Imagined

Is your life what you imagined it would be? Are you where you thought you would be at this time in your life? More and more people tell me they are not. They never imagined they would be having the financial, relationship or health difficulties they are now experiencing. They ask themselves, "What happened and why?"

There is a paradox to the phrase *living the life imagined*. When we think of living the life imagined, most, if not all of us, immediately think of that amazing, incredible, wonderful life we envision with everything we desire being fully lived and experienced. Why would we imagine anything less? We certainly wouldn't imagine a life of challenges, difficulties, and suffering. What would be the purpose in doing so? So where's the paradox? The paradox is that the life we *are* living *is* the life imagined, otherwise we would not be living it. Consider this, how much time and energy is spent imagining the wonderful life we desire? On occasion maybe, when we are a little down, when we are experiencing frustration. Perhaps when we see something or have an experience that feels incredibly good. Maybe when you see someone else living in a particular way and you wonder what it might feel like to live as that person lives.

Now consider how much time is spent imagining the challenges, worries, and concerns of each day, week, or month. How much time is spent on what might happen, especially when what might happen could be unpleasant? How often do you catch yourself in fearful thought? Don't get me wrong: I am not suggesting you have these thoughts intentionally; it is just where thoughts tend to go when unattended.

When we imagine life's challenges and difficulties we not only think they are possible but are inevitable. Our imagination is so powerful that when we imagine these events taking place we actually feel the fear, sadness, and angst of the experience even though the event has yet to take place. We also do the same with past events. We bring forward the feelings of that past experience as though it were happening now.

Just for a moment try this experiment. Imagine a happy, joyful time in your life. A time when you were full of joy, full of happiness, full of, well, Life. As you relive this experience, how do you feel? Are you not full of the joy, happiness and sense of well-being that you experienced during the actual event?

If you want to try this experiment with a sad or difficult event from your history by all means do so, however I say why bother? Life in the present moment can be challenging enough without our consciously calling forth an experience from the past when we felt sadness, grief or fear.

Why is it that even though we know we are capable of creating an experience that has either been pulled from the past or the future we are reluctant or unwilling to accept the truth that we are responsible for how we create and experience life in the present moment? In the experiment we demonstrated how we can create experiences not occurring in the moment that have all of the physical aspects of it being a present moment experience. Yet we don't take advantage of our ability to consciously create the experiences of life we desire.

It is intriguing that we don't readily see and accept the truth that life is a reflection of our beliefs and subsequent thoughts about our Self and life. If a person's thoughts dwell mostly on what they perceive as challenging or difficult, his or her life experience will reflect those thoughts. Conversely, if they spend their thinking moments on the goodness of life and all it has to offer, they draw to themselves opportunities that reinforce the truth that life is good.

The intention of what was stated above isn't to imply that life will be free of challenges if we only think good thoughts. Life will present challenges (opportunities) for our personal expansion, expression and experience of Self regardless. However we compound them by investing time, energy and imagination in them. The point is that we are in charge of how and what we think. The opportunity lies in imagining and consciously creating the experiences we desire in this moment which then will result in how life is reflected to us.

When imagining life as you would like it I suggest you not just think about it. I suggest you immerse your Self in it and think from it. This is done by placing yourself in the midst of the experience—feeling it, seeing it, and experiencing all that it is within your imagination as if it already is. When we imagine our Self in the midst of an experience we see everything out of our own eyes, not as an observer who sees themselves in the experience but as the active participant who is witness to all that is happening around and within him or her.

As an example, on a regular basis I place myself in the midst of my successful coaching practice. I feel the satisfaction of knowing how someone has benefitted from our work together. I feel the sense of joy I experience doing something I love to do and for which I get paid quite well. I feel and experience the excitement of that moment when my client has that *aha* experience that from that moment forward has dramatically changed his or her life forever. I don't *think* about how they will feel or how I feel when I have this experience. I *feel* the way I feel when I am having the experience even though it is being experienced through my imagination.

It is in consciously investing in these creative moments in our Self that we receive the dividend of living the life imagined. Note that I said *consciously* investing. Whether we do or don't imagine consciously, the result is the same: we live the life imagined. Using your imagination costs nothing. Not using your imagination can cost the experience of life you desire and that is fully available to you.

"It is not a question of whether or not you can live the life you imagine; the question is, will it be from conscious creation or default?"

Let your imagination run wild. Imagine extravagantly. Imagine beyond the bounds of what is believed reasonable or possible. Whatever you imagine contains the potential to be. Everything we desire from life has always been available, is now fully available and will always be fully available in this and every moment. All we have to do is consciously imagine what we desire, acknowledge (gratitude) that all we desire is available and then allow all we desire to flow to us.

"And, when you want something, all of the Universe conspires in helping you to achieve it."

—Paulo Coelho, The Alchemist

Chapter 7

Living In Full Expression (LIFE)

Our fullest expression and grandest experience of Self comes from the union of our human spirit and Divine Spirit working and creating together. It is by living in full expression of these aspects of our Self that we create and experience a world that can hold peace and peacefulness. And it is in living in full expression of these aspects of our Self that we come to know our Self as Divinity.

"Living in full expression is the process of allowing that which we are to be fully experienced and expressed."

Living in full expression is allowing this sacred union to be fully expressed and experienced within our experiences of life. It is being curious, excited, vulnerable, creative, loving, receptive and grateful. It is being bold and courageous; a willingness to open oneself to receive and experience all life has to offer. It is experiencing our Self as we choose to experience and express our Self in each moment, fully, completely and wholly (holy).

"Within each moment is the experience of our full expression."

A word that comes up quite often around the topic of living in full expression is *authentic* or *authenticity*. A definition of *authentic* that truly speaks to its application as intended in this material is "not corrupt from the original (source)." With this definition in mind, how do you answer the question, "Who am I?" Who or what do you believe your Self to be? One of the definitions consistently used of who we are is that we are an "individuated expression of the Divine." We are an expression or extension of the Divine, or God, or Spirit living on Earth in human form. As an individuated expression of the Divine we are here to explore, express, and experience the fullness of our divinity. As an expression of the Divine, the Divine experiences and expresses itself through our expression and experience of Self. Therefore, as we live in full expression the Divine is in full expression.

"In Truth we are the Divine clothed in humanity."

When we live in full expression we are true to ourselves, expressing who we know our Self to be in that moment. It is allowing who we are, our authentic Self, our Divine Self to be seen, enjoyed, embraced, experienced, and appreciated by all. And more importantly, it is our seeing, enjoying, embracing, experiencing, and appreciating our Self for who we are now, and who we are in the process of being.

In a workshop I conduct, participants are asked a question that has deep meaning and purpose when answered honestly: What do you want others to know about you before you die that they don't already know? As you read this question, what feelings or emotions immediately surface for you? Does an answer quickly come to mind?

Workshop attendees were asked to write down their answers, pair up with someone they didn't know and then share their answers. What resulted was not a surprise. Less than 50 percent came up with an answer. Because the number was relatively small I suggested they consider the question over the course of the next few days to see what, if anything, came to mind.

I was excited to receive several e-mails from participants in the ensuing days of the workshop stating that they had in fact come up with something they had a strong desire to express or share. They also stated that they had not contemplated anything like this until they were asked the question and took the time to deeply consider an answer.

We all have some aspect of our Self that is longing to be expressed and experienced, something significant and meaningful to our greater understanding and experience of Self.

Something the Divine desires to experience or express through our expression. Why is it that we deny this sacred part of ourselves? What is it we fear so greatly that causes us to bury so deeply what we long to express and experience? Could it be that we are afraid of our own magnificence and the responsibility we attach to being magnificent? Answering a few questions can provide insight into why we hold back this expression.

The first question is, "Am I *willing* to share or, better yet, fully express and experience this part of me?" This is a very important question in the process of living in full expression. We can desire others to know something about us that we hold as important or sacred and yet be unwilling to share it. This unwillingness can stem from fear of what others might think or say, or it could be a belief we hold about the importance or relevance of what we desire to share. If you find you are unwilling or a bit hesitant about revealing this part of yourself, simply ask why. Why am I unwilling to share this part of me? What is it I fear will happen?

In Truth it doesn't matter what others think or how they might perceive us. What matters is how we feel, what we believe, and how we experience and express our Self by sharing what we are compelled to share. Sometimes revealing to our Self what we have a strong desire to express gives us the courage to finally do so.

"The only opinion of me that truly matters is the opinion I hold of my Self."

The next question; What *will* I do today, in this moment, to fully express this aspect of me that longs to be expressed? What will I do to fully express and experience this aspect of me that is vital to LIFE? (Living In Full Expression)

The final component of this exercise is for the participants to be fully aware of their feelings while sharing what they long to share, especially feelings about the Self. This part of the exercise is both expansive and liberating. We expand our experience and knowing of Self while freeing our Self from doubts and fears that have held us back. Additionally, when people are given a safe environment in which to share something they hold as important or sacred they develop the confidence and courage to do so in other areas of their life.

What does the exercise have to do with living in full expression? Quite honestly, everything. First and foremost, it requires us to think deeply about what is most important to us and about us that others don't know. It opens the way for that deep exploration of Self and offers the opportunity to express and experience this knowing with the world. By identifying that part of Self and expressing it we are *being* true to our Self.

My Turn

Of course, turnabout is fair play. Since I had asked the question of the attendees they felt it only fair that I share what I desired others to know about me. Because I have given it considerable thought I can answer without hesitation. In fact, the writing of this book, the workshops I conduct, and the coaching I do, are all expressions of what I want others to know about me before I die. I have this strong desire to see all of us, all of humanity, living in peace, living in joy, sharing the goodness of this planet with one another without judgment and without fear. This desire has been persistent as I have struggled to come to terms with who I am.

I have questioned why I have the thoughts that I have. Why I have made the choices I have made, and why I have had the experiences I have had (in fact, created). What I have now come to accept is that it was all in preparation for this moment of being comfortable with who I am. Comfortable enough to express all that I am and experience all that I am. What I want others to know about me before I die is that I have a deep passion and strong desire for all of us to know and live in full expression of who we are. I can't explain the source of this desire any more than I can explain the joy I experience in seeing others, including myself, living in full expression.

What I know is that the desire to live in full expression is in every one of us. As each one of us allows that fullest, grandest expression and experience of Self, we demonstrate who we are and what we are capable of creating and experiencing. By living in full expression we not only answer the question of what we want others to know about us, but we fulfill our Soul's desire as well. My desire to share and experience this aspect of myself is a longing that has patiently and persistently waited to be expressed. In fact, I know the desire to express much of what is presented in this book is what I desired to express in previous lifetimes. The longing is awareness that I did not complete that expression and experience even though the opportunity to do so was always present. I chose not to fully express and experience this aspect of Self because of what was happening in the world and within me during those lifetimes.

I am not suggesting that my life today is the fulfillment of previous lifetimes, for it is not. Each life I have lived was lived in full expression and experience of who I knew my Self to be in each lifetime. What I know is that no matter how many lifetimes it takes, we all ascend to the grandest expression and experience of Self while on the Earth plane. We come to know, accept and experience our Self as who we truly are, an expression of the Divine (Heaven on Earth).

When we express what longs to be expressed we invite other forms of Self-expression. When we give ourselves permission to express and experience our Self in certain ways it provides the confidence and courage to joyfully express and experience our Self in many more ways. There isn't just one expression waiting to be released throughout life. One expression opens the door for the next and so on. It is through this process of LIFE that we remember, express and experience our Divinity.

Living Life Conditionally

I invite you to engage in an exercise throughout the course of the next day or so. Take note of the thoughts you have that are telling you to be, do or say something to appease someone else, to conform, to not rock the proverbial boat. These might be thoughts you have or actions you take out of fear for what others might think, say or do if you don't do what is expected of you. It could be your fear of the perceived consequences of an action you might take that prevents you from taking that action. Write them down for future reference and pay particular attention to any patterns that are revealed.

The stress and suffering we experience in life is in response to our resistance to life. It is our unwillingness to accept life as it shows up, and our unwillingness to speak our truth when it longs to be expressed. Life is experienced in the moment, yet we take ourselves out of the moment with our worries, concerns, thoughts and beliefs. Life is not a competition it is a collaboration. When we recognize and accept this truth we will see that life returns to us what we give to it.

Your life is your life to live as you decide to live it. In spite of outside influences you are always at a point of choice as to the direction of your life. Are your choices leading you toward the life experiences you desire or are they taking you off course and therefore further away from the life you desire? After all is said and done you are the ultimate authority in your life.

What if you didn't feel the need to be a certain way to be accepted by others? What if you lived life fully expressing who you are without concern for what others might think or say? What if you lived in the moment, free of all worries or concerns about what might happen and gave your Self permission to create and experience what you desire? Would you feel liberated?

I know for many this might conjure thoughts of a society in constant turmoil. But I have to ask, how is the way we are living now working? Why are so many of us dissatisfied with the way our lives are unfolding? Why do so many, if not most, feel there has to be a better way? Why have we *chosen* to suffer as we do?

Most are probably familiar with the concept of *free will.* Free will is one of the greatest gifts we have been given as human beings, but we don't fully exercise it. Think for a minute about a fear or concern you have about what others might say or think or what you believe might happen if you take certain actions. Does this fear or concern prevent you from taking that action and therefore not creating the experience you desire? All too often we don't do or don't say what we truly desire to say out of this fear. And yet, free will says we can do or say anything we want at any time. The only things holding us back are our thoughts, beliefs and fears of what might result.

There is no question that society imposes conditions upon us that are intended for our best interest, safety and to maintain order. There is etiquette we follow to honor and respect others just as we would have them honor and respect us. However, the conditions about which I am speaking are those self-imposed conditions we accept that deny our living in full expression of our truth.

Let's look at someone working at a job they really dislike, perhaps it's you. The truth is, quitting is an option. Now you might say, "No, I can't quit this job because I have bills to pay and a family to feed and to support. What would my family think if I just quit?" And so on and so on and so on. All of these responsibilities might be true, but the fact remains, you can quit this job. The consequences of doing so might not be ones you are willing to face. However, quitting the job is an option.

What if it really isn't the job that is the issue but your thoughts and beliefs about the job or the people with whom you work? What if you felt free to address the issues as you see them, to speak openly about what is bothering you without fear of reprisal? What if what you perceive as issues are not real issues but just your perception or misunderstanding?

When I say *living in full expression* we are not to ignore or disrespect the opinions of others. Instead just recognize that their opinions are based on their perspective of life and have nothing whatsoever to do with us. We are going to encounter differing opinions, however this doesn't make them wrong and us right, or vice versa. It means that what they believe or what we believe is what each understands as the truth in that moment. We are to respect each other for who we are, knowing that each is doing the best they can with what they know (remember) and have experienced to this moment on their journey.

You might very well make a decision to stay at a job because you believe it offers the best opportunity for you at this moment. The key is that you are consciously deciding to stay, not out of a sense of obligation or condition but because you have chosen to do so. When we make decisions based on what others say we need to do or what they believe is possible we subordinate our personal power. When we subordinate our personal power we are in Self-denial of the truth of who we are and of what we are capable of creating and experiencing.

The point in this simple example is that we remain in uncomfortable, stressful situations because we think we have no other choice. We are afraid of what we perceive to be the consequences of any decision we might make. We believe that what life has brought us is somehow all that we deserve. And yet, there are always options available to us.

Here's another perspective. What if the discomfort you are feeling is your Soul nudging you to make a change? What if this is your guidance to get you out of what you are currently doing in order to more fully express and experience who you are? What if this is the opportunity you have been waiting for to finally explore and experience the passions that have been incessantly burning within you for as long as you can remember?

We are here on this planet to gain a greater understanding of our Self. We are here to trust our Self. We are here to have the most complete and expansive experience of our Self possible through our Self-expression. I am not suggesting you quit your job, although you might. What I am suggesting is that you consider how you limit your experience of Self by not exercising your free will. As it is, most of us live conditional lives. We have become too concerned and too comfortable with what others think, do and say. We have been living according to conditions imposed upon us by others that we have come to accept.

The time is now to step to the edge of the cliff and take that joyful leap into uncertainty, knowing that we will land in our magnificence.

We know we are in full expression by how we feel and the way life flows to and through us. We are not caught up in the drama of life. We observe and embrace life. We look at every situation, challenging or otherwise, as another opportunity to explore and express who we are, who we desire to be and who we are in the process of being (becoming). We live without judgment towards one another or life itself. We allow each Soul to fully express and experience its Self on its own terms without conditions.

Chapter 8

Living an Enriched Life

Enrich (ĕn-rĭch'): To make fuller, more meaningful, rewarding or fulfilling, to add greater value or significance. In other words, it is the expansion and enhancement of what already is. In terms of living in full expression, it is the expansion and enhancement of our concept of Self, who we know our Self to be, and then living from that knowing.

Consider what it would be like to live an enriched life. How might your life be changed? How might you think, feel or act toward your Self and others? How might you experience the events of your life differently from your experience of them now? How would it feel to live life with more meaning, joy, and fulfillment? What would it mean to trust your Self completely under all situations and circumstances?

Take a few minutes to contemplate these questions. As you do, consider different areas of your life, such as relationships, career, spirituality, health, family, and finances. What can you do within each of these areas of your life to create a richer, fuller and more rewarding experience? Better yet, what are you *willing* to do to create these enriched experiences?

"Living an enriched life isn't about changing life's events; it's changing how we perceive and experience life's events."

An enriched life is a life of purpose, passion, joy and happiness. It is accepting responsibility for one's life and making choices in alignment with what one desires to experience and express. We trust in our Self and life to present exactly what we need to live in full expression. We accept challenges as opportunities for the grandest expansion, expression, and experience of Self. This simple change in how we perceive life's events brings peace and calm that support us through all of life's experiences.

Some might question how a life can be enriched by someone faced with a sudden physically disabling injury, a serious illness, or a devastating personal financial crisis. The answer is twofold. First, individuals coping with challenging life experiences will enrich their own life by how they meet and experience the challenge. They might experience criticism, fear or judgment. However, they will also experience an outpouring of love, support and compassion, all of which enriches life. Secondly, our lives will be enriched by observing how courageously these Souls accept the challenging experience. How we perceive the experience presents an opportunity for a grander experience and expression of our Self.

We must keep in mind that we don't know, and perhaps never will know or understand, the life path another Soul has chosen. Blessing, honoring, respecting and supporting them as they go through the experience, regardless of how difficult or painful it might seem, enriches the experience for all.

This was brought home for me one day as I was waiting to get my hair cut. A middle-aged mother was getting her hair styled while her severely physically challenged son sat beside her in his wheelchair. He was restrained to prevent his slumping over and could only grunt and make guttural noises. From time to time, the mom would reach out, touch her son in a playful way and make a comment I was unable to hear. Each time she did so he responded with a smile and a noise only the mom understood. She continued playing with him, making him laugh and move around wildly in his wheel chair, which caused her to laugh. As I watched the two of them I remember thinking that this was one of the most amazing and beautiful displays of love I had ever witnessed.

My experience of this event caused me to express gratitude for the many blessings I have been given. It also caused me to express gratitude for the experience of seeing such love expressed. I don't know why this young man chose to enter this world in that body but I do know my life was enriched because he did.

Living an enriched life brings greater awareness, appreciation, acceptance, joy and feeling to life. There is a greater sense of connectedness with all things, a greater understanding of the balance, harmony, and perfection of all things. An enriched life is bolder, more expressive, and more alive. We courageously share, express, and experience our authentic Self. We allow the authentic *me* to emerge and freely experience the fullness of every moment.

"The more we enrich our own lives,
the more we enrich the lives of others.
The more we enrich the lives of others,
the more we enrich our own."

We typically look at a relationship in terms how we "believe" the other person makes us feel. In truth, it is not how the other person makes us feel that enriches the relationship or any other aspect of life.

It is our relationship with our Self and what we believe and feel about our Self that enriches the relationship and therefore life. It is essential that we allow our feelings to be expressed in all areas of life as they are the essence of enrichment. The more we access and allow these feelings the more available they become. The more we allow and experience our feelings the more alive we become. The more alive we are the more life is enriched.

Life is enriched through our expanding awareness and experience of who we are and desire to be. It is through the window of awareness that we see the limitless potential of life. An enriched life is the most rewarding life possible for it fulfills the promise of the grandest expression and experience of Self.

Chapter 9

Miracles

Miracles are defined as experiences or events for which we have no logical understanding or explanation. They are usually attributed to religious, spiritual, God or otherworldly figures. Those to whom miracles have been credited did not create them as demonstrations of what they were capable of doing, but as demonstrations of who we are and of what each of us is capable of creating. *These things and much more will you do.*

As an aspect of the Divine we are here to experience our Self as a creator. Miracles, plain and simple are acts of creation, whether consciously created or by default. We consciously create miracles through our awareness and intention to create what we desire to experience. Miracles created by default are those that are the result of subconscious thoughts and beliefs, primarily about our Self.

It is easy to understand and accept every event and experience of life as a miracle when we consider all that has to come together for any event or experience to take place. Every choice we have made has resulted in every experience we have had in this and previous lifetimes. But it doesn't stop there. Every experience we have is also the result of all of the choices made by those with whom we share an experience. The intricacies and complexity of life's events are far beyond human comprehension or logical explanation, therefore making them miracles.

We have to understand and accept that we are part of the creation process here on Earth. We are in partnership with the Universe, the Divine, and the creative force behind all that is. Even though we might not have an awareness of our role in the creation of each experience, we are in fact responsible for the experiences we have. I don't believe we are responsible for each event that takes place for there are random occurrences on the Earth plane; however, our experience of each event is our responsibility (ability to respond). We choose how we will respond to each life event resulting in the experience we have of that event, or more precisely, our experience of our Self within the context of the event.

When the conditions are such the miracle occurs. Nothing comes into existence if the conditions for the creation are not perfect for its creation. This applies to everything, including our belief in what is possible. If we don't believe what we desire is possible, then it is not. If we doubt that what we desire will come to be, then it will not. This is perhaps one of the toughest conditions to meet. We have been so programmed as to what we can and cannot do that we have difficulty letting go of limiting beliefs and therefore limit our experience as creators.

Nature is the perfect expression of miracles occurring when conditions are such. I have long marveled at how one day there are no mushrooms in my backyard and then the next there are mushrooms standing three or four inches tall. We can rationalize and get into the biology of how mushrooms grow but the point is that they grow because the conditions for their creation and existence are perfect. One day the conditions are not perfect and then the next they are and we have mushrooms.

The same is true with anything we want to create or desire to experience. The conditions for our desire must be such that the experience is created. The conditions include all that we can do physically, but more importantly, it is the requirement of letting go of anything that would deny the experience we are in the process of creating. These include any doubts, fears or thoughts of unworthiness. Including any doubts or thoughts about what we desire to create being possible. I can assure you the mushroom had no doubts, fears, or thoughts of unworthiness or possibility, nor did that which created it.

My intention is to place the focus on conscious creation of the experiences we desire versus those that show up by default. First and foremost, we have to believe and accept that we are co-creators in the creation process. We have to believe that we are capable of creating miracles and in fact have been creating miracles throughout our lifetimes. We have to believe the experience we desire to create is intended and of a beneficent nature; otherwise, we would not have the inspiration in the first place.

"Believing in miracles is one thing. Believing we are capable of creating them is quite another."

Our active, conscious participation in creating miracles accomplishes two things. First, it reinforces within us the knowing that we are capable of creating the miracle we desire. Second, it sends notice to the Universe that we are serious about what it is we desire to create and experience and are receptive to the partnership we have with the Universe in the creation process. The creative force of the Universe follows the direction our conscious mind gives it by way of our thoughts, beliefs, and feelings. The creative force does whatever the conscious mind impresses upon it. Ask, and it is given. We are in union with the Universe in the act of creation. This is the collaboration and integration of the Divine Spirit with the Human spirit.

It is when we fully trust in the process, fully trust in our Self as co-creator, that life unfolds more as we desire. I use the phrase "more as we desire" instead of "completely as we desire," because there are experiences we will have that will not appear as we desired them. However, they will be exactly as we need them for the experience our Soul intended.

Humans are more comfortable and more likely to consciously engage in a process when there are specific guidelines. Here are suggested steps to facilitate the conscious creation of miracles in the current lifetime.

1. **Express gratitude** for all that you have experienced and all that is and yet to be. This is an important daily activity; however, it is especially important when intentionally creating an experience one desires. This expression of gratitude must be heart-felt and sincere. It must also include those experiences that at the time of the experience appear as hardships. How many times have you had an experience that was difficult but in hindsight you realized it was a blessing in disguise? What if you recognized every experience as a blessing in the moment and not as a blessing in hindsight? How would the experience have been different?

Expressing gratitude is a vital component of living in full expression. Living in full expression encompasses expressing and experiencing oneself as a creator. Be grateful for all that you have co-created for the grandest expression and experience of Self.

2. **Define the miracle** with as much clarity as possible. It is only when we know what we truly desire that we create and experience it. Too often we do not define what we desire with clarity and are surprised by what shows up. Take the time necessary to get as clear as possible. Align your Self with your desire and make choices that support your desire being experienced.

Anything that you desire to create or bring into your lived experience is just that: an experience. When you are clarifying what you desire, understand that what you are really trying to bring into your life is the experience you will have as a result of whatever it is you desire.

3. **What conditions must be met** in order for your miracle to occur? This is not a list of things that you believe you have to have in place before you can create your miracle. You might believe that you need a certain amount of money, and therefore delay engaging in the process until you save enough money. You might believe that you don't have time now and therefore delay engaging in the creation of the miracle until the so-called perfect time.

The miracle is the creation of the experience now without our placing any undue conditions upon it or expectations on how we believe it should appear. We are in Truth creating an experience. How it unfolds is not important. It will unfold in the perfect way it is intended to unfold.

Create the experience you desire in your mind as if the miracle has already occurred. From this experiential perspective, what took place for the miracle to occur? Look back on what has taken place that allowed you to be in the experience you desired in this moment. Of those things that took place in your mind, what can you do to facilitate the actual creation of your miracle?

a. **Assume the experience** of the experience you desire. When we assume something we regard it as true in the moment. When creating a miracle, regard the experience as if it has already taken place and what you are doing is calling it forth. When we have a thought about something we give it the potential to be (another act of creation). Think from within the experience and not about the experience. Engage all of your senses as if you are in the midst of the experience. What we accept or assume as true is created. What we are in agreement with we create. Bring the experience of the experience you desire into this aspect of the creation process and you will more readily create the lived experience.

For example, if you are actually in the midst of the experience, what do you see through your eyes? What feelings do you have? What are you thinking? What are you hearing? What is the energy within the midst of the experience? What is your experience of your Self?

b. **Take action.** Be fully engaged in the process. Actively and consciously engage in the process of your miracle's creation. Do all within your power to create your miracle and do it joyfully, passionately and enthusiastically. When we consciously engage in the process we serve notice to the Universe through our thoughts, words and deeds, that we are all in. When the Universe knows we are all in, the Universe then does it part to bring about the miracle.

c. **Have faith** that what you desire is in the process of being created and it will in fact be created. In other words, get out of the way. Allow the miracle to occur naturally. Let go of any attachment to the details, outcome or any doubt about whether or not it will be. Let the partnership play out; let the creative force of the Universe fulfill its role in the creation of the miracle.

"FAITH: fully allow it to happen."

4. **Trust.** Trust LIFE and the process of LIFE, more importantly, trust in your Self.

5. **Know that what you receive** might not be exactly what you asked for. However, it will be exactly what you need in the way it is needed.

6. **Expect and Embrace the unexpected**. If there are unexpected steps presented in the process they are for your further growth, expansion, and experience of your Self. They are an integral part of the miracle itself; otherwise they would not have been presented. Embrace the miracle as it unfolds even though it might unfold in an unexpected way. It will always unfold perfectly, regardless of appearance, for your highest and best good.

The True miracle occurs when we acknowledge and accept the creator within and allow it to create free of judgment, doubt or limitation. The True miracle is you.

Chapter 10

Living from Intention

"The way we view life, our perspective, determines how we respond to life. How we respond to life determines how we experience life. Our experience of life is a reflection of who we believe our Self to be."

What if there was a way to change your experience of life—to see life not as it appears but as the potential it promises? What if you could fully harness the power that flows through and within you? How might your life be different if you knew you were living intentionally in alignment with your Soul's mission?

All we want to be and experience will manifest when the conditions of those desires are met. Understanding and meeting those conditions begins with answering five simple, yet revealing questions. The answers to which hold the key to unlocking the potential for the life experiences of our intention.

As you answer each question consider why you answered as you did. And as you think about your response bring your attention to your feelings and consider why you feel as you do. Do I believe that what I believe creates the life I have and can experience? Why or why not?

1. Do I believe I can change my life experience(s)? Why or why not?
2. Do I have the desire to create different life experiences? Why or why not?
3. Do I have the willingness to do what is necessary to create different life experiences? Why or why not?
4. What life experiences do I want to create? Why?

Awareness

Awareness is the key. It is only when we are consciously aware that we are present and available to what is happening in the moment. The present moment is the only time in which we can make choices and create the life experiences we desire. Awareness is being present to all that is happening around and within us in any given moment. There is no effort in awareness, just an allowing of life in the moment to unfold while consciously observing all that is unfolding without judgment. Awareness is the quiet observation and experience of our connection with all things.

"Once aware, all else falls into place."

The experience of awareness is difficult to put in words because one's awareness is dependent upon what is being perceived. What is perceived is the interpretation of the experience based on one's thoughts and beliefs. As we expand our awareness through the attentive practice of awareness, we gain greater clarity of who we are in relation to life. We see the correlation of our life experiences with our thoughts and beliefs. We are empowered by the awareness of our ability and the opportunity to change our thoughts and beliefs to more align with our desires.

Be aware of your thoughts, words, and actions. Be aware of the correlation between your thoughts and beliefs and all that is happening around you and within you. Be aware of how you feel when responding to situations, circumstances, opportunities and their potential consequences.

Be aware of how you use your imagination toward the infinite potential that lies in wait. Be aware of how you express yourself. Be aware of how you experience your Self. Be aware of the relationship you have with your Self.

Be aware of who you are and desire to be in every moment. And watch with *attentive appreciation* as your life unfolds perfectly toward the grandest experience and expression of Self possible.

Awareness is essential for creating a life with intention. Out of our awareness comes the realization that perhaps we have become too comfortable in our discomfort. Without conscious awareness of what is happening within and around us we have no context for the change we desire.

Awareness as a practice can be exercised at any time of day in any environment. However, as I described my experience of being, "immersed in the silence of the dawn," I encourage you find the most conducive time and environment for you to experience and expand attentive awareness. When are you most open and receptive? When, where and how can you become quiet and still? When and where are you without distraction or interruption?

Set aside this time every day for your practice and experience of awareness and you will soon find that your "conscious awareness" expands into all areas of your life resulting in greater clarity, better choices and a higher level of personal empowerment.

As you practice awareness be aware of the following without judgment or attachment:

1. Be aware of your thoughts.
2. Be aware of your feelings.
3. Be aware of the relationship or correlation between your thoughts and feelings.
4. Be aware of the correlation between your thoughts, feeling, beliefs and the experiences life presents to you.
5. Be aware of the resistance you have to what life offers.
6. Be aware of all that is happening around you and within you.
7. Be aware of those moments when you are not aware.
8. Be aware of judgement.
9. Be aware of being aware.

"Awareness allows love, peace, joy and happiness
to be experienced and expressed.
Awareness is consciousness; we are consciousness.
Awareness allows for the grandest experience
and expression of Self.
We are at first aware, then awareness itself."

Lifting the Fog

Everything that life presents is for our continued expansion, experience, and expression of Self, regardless of how it shows up or how challenging or difficult it might appear. Being clear on how we want to experience life calls forth the potential for it to be. Clarity is one of the greatest tools of creation we have and yet it presents one of our most challenging opportunities.

Why would clarity be considered a challenging opportunity? Clarity is about removing any obstruction to our knowing who we are, what we are and what we are here to experience and express.Here's the challenge: Our clarity is clouded by our thoughts and beliefs, especially disempowering ones. They are like a dense morning fog that obscures the truth of what is in front of us. It is not until the morning sun shines brightly that the fog lifts and all that is before us is revealed. And so it is with our thoughts and beliefs. As we shine the spotlight on the validity of our thoughts and beliefs, the truth of who we are and of what we are capable of creating is revealed.

Most of us are unable to imagine and accept how powerful we are because of the difficulty we have imagining beyond the limits of our beliefs, and yet we have been endowed with the gift of imagination to do just that. We fail to use our imagination to the fullest extent possible because we don't allow ourselves the freedom to fully explore who we are, what we truly desire and what we are capable of experiencing. We don't believe that what we imagine can actually be ours.

The truth is we cannot imagine anything that does not have the potential to be. The very thought of something creates its potential. We might not know how it will come to be, and yet, if we hold it as possible its means for being will be revealed.

"Are we afraid to imagine what can be because we have imagined that it can't be?"

It is within our imagination that we first create the experiences we desire to have. Imagine your life, or any aspect of it, from the perspective of it already being everything you desire. Create (imagine) a clear picture, or more importantly, a clear sense of how it feels to enjoy this life as if you are already in the midst of the experience. And if you don't like what you have imagined, re-imagine it as the experience you truly desire.

The most important aspect of clarity is being clear on who we are. This is not the labels we assume, the roles we play, the accomplishments we have. It is not even the name by which we are known. Knowing who we are and embracing this truth is the key to opening oneself to the so called Kingdom. Once you know and accept that you are an aspect of the Divine and you live from this knowing, there is nothing you can't create and experience. Nothing. In fact, it is from this knowing that you will realize that you have been creating your life experiences all along. As you embrace this truth you open your Self to the conscious creation of the experiences you desire from this moment on.

But understand something very important, everything that has been created and experienced by you, consciously or not, has been for your benefit, regardless of how it showed up. Each experience has been an opportunity to know and experience your Self within the context of each experience. And from each experience you have the opportunity to expand your knowing of who you are and what you are capable of creating and experiencing.

From the very first thought we have about what we desire to experience the potential for it to be exists, including the thought of who we are as Divine beings. What brings forth the experience is the belief that it is possible and the willingness to be and do what is necessary for it to be realized.

Virtuous Cycle of LIFE

Clarity on what we desire to experience in life is essential if we are to consciously create it. However, clarity about who we are is what we are seeking through each experience we create. The more we create, express, and experience our Self within the context of the life events we call to our Self, the greater our knowing and experience of the Truth of who we are becomes. The greater our knowing of who we are becomes, the more we create, express and experience who we are consciously. This is the virtuous cycle of LIFE (living in full expression).

Desire

How badly do you want it? Conscious change (creation) does not take place without a desire for change. Believing we can create change is but one aspect of the creation process; having a strong desire for change is the catalyst.

Desire is that stirring within that compels us to take action. It is the energy that builds up, overpowers and replaces complacency. Desire is derived from the inspiration that flows through us. Desire moves us beyond stagnation. Desire results in our intention which provides the focus and clarity needed to bring about change. Desire is an attracting energy that facilitates the creation process, therefore change. Desire should not be confused with wanting. Desire is Divine inspiration, whereas wanting stems from a lack or need of (neediness) something. Desire pertains to the experiences of the Soul.

"When desire for change is strong enough, feelings and emotions emerge. They rise up within and serve as the inspirational force for change."

From desire we begin to change how we see and think about life. In fact, we might now see things that were always present but previously held no importance. People, information and events that support what we desire to create or experience begin to enter our awareness. We become more receptive to our surroundings and the opportunities they present. We open ourselves to potential, whereas before we saw limitation. Desire facilitates the alignment process during which the Universe conspires with us to deliver the object of our desire.

Desire is difficult to define as it must be experienced to be fully understood. Words can only point to what desire is and the effect it might have on us. The experience of desire, like all other feelings, is unique to each of us. I cannot tell you how it feels for me to desire something any more than you can tell me. However, we all know through the experience of it.

The desire we have for the change we seek is not the changing of our life events; it is changing how we experience life's events. To change how we experience life's events we need only to change how we experience ourselves. For as we perceive our Self we perceive and experience life. The inner relationship we have with our Self is reflected through our life's experiences; as within, so without.

Willingness

As you consider where you are now within your life experience and how you desire it to unfold from this point forward, consider your willingness to make it happen. Are you willing to experience all that you desire? Are you willing to do what is necessary to bring about the change? You might have the desire that brings about the opportunity; however, it is your willingness that will make it happen.

We have all had experiences in life when we had a strong desire to do something but for any number of reasons we were unwilling to do what was necessary to create it. Desire for change brings about the opportunity for change; however, it is our willingness to change that fully opens the gate.

"Unless we have a willingness to do what is necessary for what we desire it remains unfulfilled potential."

From where does willingness originate? It comes from our depth of passion for life and the quantity and quality of the life experiences we desire to have. It comes from embracing our potential, dropping limiting beliefs and thoughts, allowing and receiving all life that offers.

Willingness has no reluctance. When our depth of passion for what we desire to experience reaches the level necessary to take the appropriate steps, we do so joyfully and without hesitation. Some might say under certain circumstances the sacrifice involved is too great a price to pay, and yet when our passion runs deep enough there is no sacrifice. It is in this moment that we place far greater value on what we desire to experience than the perceived sacrifice necessary to bring it about.

Willingness is being available and receptive to change. It requires one to be vulnerable and bold, open to new ideas, new information, and in most instances, new ways of thinking, seeing, and acting. It is once again acknowledging that what we see as truth today might not be true tomorrow. It is our willingness to relinquish what has not and does not serve us in our desire for richer, more rewarding life experiences. Willingness requires that we live from our imaginations, not our memories. Willingness invites us to step into the uncertainty and magnificence of what lies before us and within us.

"Whatever you can do or dream you can, begin it.
Boldness has genius, power and magic in it."

—Goethe

Uncertainty turns in our favor when we imagine and hold thoughts of what we desire to experience and consciously make choices towards the realization of those experiences. It is when we know we are moving toward something that is beneficial that we are more likely and more willing to take the steps necessary to bring it about.

If you are inspired to do something but find you are unwilling to do what is required to bring your inspiration to life, question why. Why am I unwilling to do what I have such a strong desire to create and experience? Why am I denying my Self this opportunity to experience and express my Self through this inspiration?

The answers to these questioning are limiting beliefs you hold about your Self. They are what prevent you from fully stepping into and experiencing your magnificence, the truth of who you are.

To Be Inspired is to Be Alive

One of the greatest gifts we have to offer one another, and therefore the world, is to live in full expression of who we truly are. When we live in full expression we not only give our Self permission to live boldly, confidently and joyfully through that which makes us come alive, but we give others permission and the confidence to come alive as well.

Being alive in this world means that we are honoring and respecting the Soul based inspirations we are given. We acknowledge the passion and desire that has built up within us that yearns to be expressed. We allow the expression and experience of our inspirations to see and feel the freedom of being released in to the world while liberating us from the limiting beliefs we have held to this moment that prevented our full expression.

"Be responsible to your inspirations."

So why is it that we withhold such a magnificent experience from and of our Self? Why would we deny (Self-denial) the world the full experience of who we truly are? A primary reason is we don't trust the inspiration we have been given. We think it is just a passing fancy that feels good when we are first inspired, but by lunchtime we convince ourselves that that which we were earlier inspired to create and experience is not worthwhile or achievable.

"We accept life as it is instead of what it can be."

An inspiration is a desire of the Soul that allows the Divine to be in full expression of its Self through us. And yet, it is only we who can grant permission for this full expression. Too often we become too comfortable in our discomfort to move towards that which would give us the greatest comfort of all. We become convinced that life as we are living it is life as it was intended to be, at least for us. We believe others are more deserving of the goodness of life.

"Life is an equal opportunity experience.
It withholds nothing from anyone."

We might think there is too much risk involved in moving out of the comfort of our discomfort towards something as ethereal as an inspiration. However, the greatest risk is in not taking the joyous leap of faith toward that which our Soul desires.

"We would not be inspired to do
something if it was not intended to be.
If it is intended to be, all for it to be is provided."

To be inspired means to breathe life into. Accept and honor your inspirations by breathing life into them. Be bold and courageous by answering the call of your Soul. When you do, you give notice to the Universe that you are all in. When the Universe knows you are all in it responds accordingly by supporting you in the full expression and experience of that inspiration. When you accept the invitation of an inspiration you become fully alive and engaged in the process of creating the greatest experience and expression of your Self possible, your very reason for being here.

"When you breathe Life into that
for which you have been inspired,
Life is breathed into you."

FAITH

Faith is an important aspect of the creation process. It is after we have created the virtual reality through our imagination and belief that with faith it will manifest. In fact, the word faith contains within its letters instructions of what we are to do.

"Fully Allow It To Happen."

In other words, get out of the way and let the forces behind creation take full effect. There is a knowing and trusting when we see faith in this way. We do what we can do and then we trust, have FAITH, that what we desire will become manifest.

When we change how we see things from the way they appear to the potential of what can be we open the way for a different experience. It begins by acknowledging and accepting the power we have to effect change. This power lies in our ability to choose. We are presented with the opportunity to make a choice in every situation whether conscious of it or not. We either make intentional (conscious) choices based on what we want to create and experience or we make reactive (unconscious) choices based on past experiences, memory and fear. Our past experiences and memories do not tell us who or where we are; they tell us who and where we have been. It is our history to this moment—nothing more, nothing less. It is only in this moment, now, that we can make choices that create new experiences that become our history as we continue our journey. Life is the autobiography we write as it is lived.

"The past does not equal the future."

The above statement is true if we choose for it to be true. However, the past can equal the future if we consistently bring the past to the present moment. If we continue to believe that what happened in the past is somehow fixed or permanent and a determining factor in what can or will happen now, we will continue to create those experiences. If we continue reliving the past, the past will not only equal the future, it will equal our now.

Knowing that the past is nothing more than the experiences of our life is empowering. Knowing we have the power in every moment to choose how life will be experienced from this moment on means accepting responsibility for those choices. This can be frightening because in essence what we are declaring by accepting responsibility is that we no longer have any excuses for why things are the way they are. We have the power, the responsibility and the freedom to choose how we will experience the now.

As we accept responsibility for our choices we also accept responsibility for our experiences. When we believe in our personal power to create positive change and we have faith that what we desire to experience will come to be, we clear the way for creating continuous, conscious change.

Chapter 11

The Goodness of LIFE

When we live in full expression of that which we are, we create, experience and contribute to the richness and fullness of life in all of its expressions. We are in alignment with our pure essence and allow it to be expanded, expressed, and experienced.

Living in full expression has many aspects to it. It begins with the awareness and acceptance of the infinite potential of life. It is in knowing that God (Universe) desires that we experience happiness, health, and well-being. Living in full expression is trusting in this desire and navigating life based on this trust. When we accept that happiness, health and well-being are our birthright we open ourselves to receiving and experiencing them.

Receptivity is something to which we pay little attention. We have been told throughout our lives it is better to give than receive and therefore we deny ourselves much of what is available to us. And yet, if we are not receptive to all that life presents we will not receive the full benefit of all life has to offer.

"Open yourself to receive all that life is presenting and you will be given all that life has to offer."

When we are receptive to what others give us we give them one of the greatest gifts we have to offer: the gift of giving. How do you feel when you give? If you are like most you feel a sense of satisfaction, joy and happiness that you have benefitted another person. You feel good about your Self. Doesn't it stand to reason that those who would give to you would feel the same way? When we are not receptive, we not only deny our Self the gift of what is being given, we deny the giver the opportunity to feel good about their Self for having given.

Receptivity applies to being open to love, appreciation, kindness and acceptance of Self and all that life has to offer. The greatest relationship we are here to explore and experience is our relationship with Self. This experience is inclusive of love, appreciation, kindness, respect and acceptance toward and of Self.

When we are not receptive to the goodness of life we deny what GOD or the Universe is offering. In so doing we are in judgment of our Self. On some level we have created a belief that we are not worthy of the goodness of life. This might stem from the thought that to be worthy of what the Universe has to offer there is something we are to do or some way in which we are to act or live. There might be a feeling or belief we have not done enough or worked hard enough to be rewarded with the goodness of life. On the other end of the spectrum maybe we did something that we label as bad or wrong and therefore believe we are not deserving of the goodness of life.

The Truth is there is nothing one has to do to be deserving of the goodness of life other than to be on this planet. There literally is nothing one has to do other than to accept and be who they are. Every Soul that incarnates has the right and the opportunity to experience the goodness of life. The goodness of life is not something we have to earn; it is how *we choose* to experience life.

There is a tendency in humanity to default to thoughts and beliefs that tell us what we can't do, shouldn't do or are not worthy of experiencing. It is a simple matter of awareness. Be aware of and acknowledge the thoughts you have or beliefs you hold that in any way limit your experience of life. Be aware of the overwhelming evidence that proves you are capable, deserving, and worthy of every experience of life and Self you desire. Look upon experiences you have had that reinforce the truth that you are capable of creating the experiences you desire. Set this evidence as your default point so each time you question or doubt your Self you fall back on these truths of who you are and of what you are capable.

I have found I can move beyond, or at the very least lessen, the influence of limiting thoughts and beliefs by answering a few questions.

1. Is what I am thinking and believing about my Self true? Initially you might say the belief is true, however when you consider the origin of the belief, why you believe this about your Self, you will discover more often than not it came from outside of your Self. And then you ask:
2. Is it really true or is it something I have come to accept as true? What we accept as true becomes our truth even though it might not actually be true. And then you ask:
3. What evidence is there that it is true? What hard proof do I have that this belief is true? Not because someone said it is true or that I had an experience in the past that would lead me to believe it is true, but proof that this is *always* true about me.
4. What evidence do I have that proves otherwise? What experiences have I had that prove the limiting thought or belief

is not true and therefore an illusion? It only takes one such experience because if something is the Truth it is always true.

What you will reveal in answering these questions is that you have in fact had experiences that prove you are capable and worthy of whatever you desire to experience now. The more aware you are of these truths the more open and receptive you are to all life has to offer. The more open and receptive you are to all life has to offer the more life bestows upon you.

By releasing your grip on your limiting beliefs you are free to grab more truthful, liberating beliefs. Notice I said *your grip on limiting beliefs*. Limiting beliefs do not hold onto you. They are the beliefs that you hold on to, as such they can only be released by you. The only power your beliefs have is the power you give them.

Denying What is Inherently Ours

Knowing and accepting that God, the Universe, Spirit desires us to experience happiness, health, and well-being and that life presents all that is necessary for the experience begs a question. Why would anyone deny it? Why do people consciously deny what is inherently theirs?

It begins with one's core belief of whether the Universe conspires against them or works with them. Do I believe the Universe is working to hold me back or do I believe the Universe and I are in partnership facilitating my growth and expansion, and therefore my full expression? Do I believe myself to be the beneficiary of life or a victim of life?

There are no victims. Let me repeat this, there are no victims. We are all beneficiaries of life. Any experience people have of being a victim, the belief that life and the Universe are somehow against them, is the result of their belief they are a victim. I admit this is difficult to understand and accept, especially when one is going through a personal tragedy or we observe what is happening throughout the world. Victimhood as I am describing it here is not the same as when someone suffers from an adverse act or circumstances that causes harm in one form or another.

Many events appear to be contrary to what we would consider beneficial or empowering. And yet, when we reflect on what happened we see there is always something of benefit for personal spiritual growth and expansion, as well as the spiritual growth and expansion of humanity. We often say after a trying time that we would not change the experience because it was a blessing in disguise. Knowing and believing that everything is a blessing is what allows us to experience joy and happiness in the face of adversity.

As a point of clarification I am not suggesting that experiencing joy and happiness in the face of adversity means we are joyful or happy about a devastating event like the death of a loved one or an earthquake that takes the lives of thousands. Joy and happiness are about the inner peace, the inner knowing that despite all we experience and see in the outer world all is well and we are loved beyond measure. It is out of this love that all is provided to fully express and experience who we are and are in the process of being. Unfortunate events bring to our life experiences the untold and unexpressed love and compassion we hold for one another. Within these events is an opportunity for expressing our love, joy, happiness, and gratitude for all we have.

When we accept that we chose to be here at this time and place and that every experience is for our spiritual growth and expansion, we approach events and experiences from an empowering perspective versus a disempowering perspective. Life empowers us to be, experience and express who we are fully, completely and perfectly.

Being and living in full expression is allowing life in all of its forms to flow to and through us. It is being grateful for everything life presents, including the experiences we label challenging or devastating. The thought or belief that we are victims is replaced by the knowing that we are the beneficiaries of life and all it has to offer. And all that life has to offer is for our spiritual and personal growth and expansion, and ultimately, the grandest experience and expression of Self.

Each moment offers the opportunity to choose who we are, who we desire to be, and who we are in the process of being. We choose how to experience life through the full expression of who we are.

Is it God's Will?

The Lord's Prayer states, "thy will be done on Earth as it is in heaven." What does this mean? How can we know? Do we spend time thinking about it or do we just accept that that which shows up must be God's Will? Attributing everything that happens to God's Will is an easy and available excuse for not taking responsibility for one's life. It implies judgment where one person is more deserving than another and is therefore given more of the goodness of life. It gives away our personal power as the creative Divine beings that we are. People all over this planet are waiting for God to tell them what to do instead of taking responsibility for creating the life experiences they desire. And when something challenging happens they act as if there is nothing they can do about their circumstances because it must be God's Will. I question why God would will that any of us suffer?

We make life more difficult than it needs to be or was intended to be, (simplexities). For some reason we tend to think that if something is simple there isn't as much value or worth to it, and certainly when we think of God's Will it must be more than what I suggest. I will answer the question of what is God's Will by asking a few questions. As you consider my answers I ask that you do so with an open mind. Remember: "*today what I know to be true, tomorrow might not be.*"

You might be familiar with this statement that was found in ancient texts: "As above, so below. As within, so without." What I understand it to mean is that everything exists in the macrocosm as it does in the microcosm and vice versa. As it happens on one level it happens on all levels. In other words, as in Heaven so on Earth. As it happens in our thoughts and through our imagination, it happens on Earth in our lived experience. As it happens in our heart, it happens in our world. For our purpose here we will accept that what happens in Heaven, your concept of Heaven, is intended to happen on Earth, and in fact can, will, and does.

Think of our relationship to God, referred to as our Father and we as the children of God—not some of us, but all of us. As a parent, regardless of whether or not you have children, what would you will for your children? What life experiences do you most desire? What is your will for humanity? For me, after all is said and done I want to experience, express and extend joy, happiness, love, peace, health, and well-being. I desire this for my family, my friends, and humanity. I believe this is what we all desire, regardless of differing opinions, life perspectives and religions.

If this is what we would will for our children, ourselves and for humanity, why would we think or believe that our Father, God, would will or provide anything less for us? Does it really matter how we and our children would come to experience and enjoy these things? Does it matter what line of work any of us are in? Does it matter in which part of the world we live or the type of house we own or rent? Does it matter to which religious group we belong?

You might think that this is an oversimplification of what many consider a very complex topic that we are not supposed to understand. However, I would suggest that it has to be simple so we can understand it. What good is it to say we will live so *thy will* is done if we don't know what *thy will* is? God's Will is that we live in full expression and experience of who we truly are. It is God's Will that we enjoy health, peace, joy, happiness, love and well-being as we live in full expression and experience of Self. As we are in full expression and experience of Self, God/Divinity is in full experience and expression.

I recently came across a statement regarding *will* that suggested we are to relinquish personal will for God's Will to be done. I believe we are much better served by relinquishing the thought that there is a difference between God's Will and our will. I believe we have a much better chance of God's Will being done by accepting the truth that our will and God's Will are one and the same. This belief alleviates any resistance or internal conflict we might experience when considering what life choices to make. Knowing *we* desire the same things in life and from life frees us to make choices that result in the life experiences of happiness, joy, health, peace, love and well-being. *As above, so below* extends to all aspects of life on the Earth plane, including and perhaps most importantly, the creative process in which we play an integral role as co-creators. The most intriguing and exciting part of this is that through the gift of free will we choose how *thy will* is done. We choose how to live so we experience joy, happiness, health, peace, love and well-being. We co-create the experiences of our life so we can enjoy the grandest experience and expression of Self.

Living in full expression is living in accordance with the "joint will" (that of the Divine and us) of joy, happiness, love, peace and well-being. When each of us live in full expression we are a demonstration to others of the incredible goodness of life, the potential of life and the depth of God's love and desire for us.

Heaven on Earth

Heaven on Earth: is it really possible? Or is it an elusive dream to which we attach our hope and faith? Are we here to actually experience Heaven on Earth or is it nothing more than a phrase we use to describe an event or experience that is beyond words or description? Why is it we make reference to those things we enjoy, love, or see as extraordinarily beautiful or moving as being *like* Heaven on Earth? How can we compare one experience to another if we haven't had the experience? Or have we? Is this an example of how we cannot long for something for which we have not had the experience?

What would be your experience of Heaven? What ideas, thoughts, and beliefs do you hold of Heaven? Where do they come from? Notice I used the word *experience* when asking about Heaven. This was intentional because Heaven is an experience and not a place. How can you have the experience of Heaven you hold in your thoughts and beliefs while living on the Earth plane?

Those who have had a near-death experience (NDE) describe their experience as one of intense light, love, and grandeur; of being at a place and then not being at that place; of a sudden awareness of being elsewhere in the experience. They sense being nowhere and yet everywhere simultaneously. They speak of being nothing and yet of being everything. They speak of the vividness of colors, the clarity with which they see and experience everything within their experience of heaven. They speak of the intense, indescribable, unconditional love of and from God, Jesus, Allah or whomever or whatever they believe to be the Supreme Being or force in the Universe. They describe buildings, people, animals, mountains, flowers, rivers, and canyons in terms of their magnificence, beauty, and illumination. They speak of an intensity of peace, joy and love that is beyond our human capacity to understand much less describe.

There is no awareness of the limitations they believe and hold about themselves while living in the Earth plane. They are fully immersed in the experience of Heaven with no thoughts about anything, yet a knowing of everything. There are no boundaries, no defining lines, no beginning or end. They are not doing anything yet experience the connection to everything. They are not who they thought themselves to be; they experience who they know themselves to be. They are fully immersed in the experience of being connected to, and a part of, everything simultaneously. Could it be that Heaven on Earth is the realization and acceptance of the inherent beauty and magnificence of all that we are, all that we have, and all that we experience? Is Heaven on Earth the unconditional love of Self, of life, and all it has to offer? Could it be we gain the clarity of those that have had a NDE when we open ourselves to the magnificence of our Self, to life, and accept that God's Will is that we have this experience in this and every incarnation? Could it be that the *experience* of Heaven on Earth is living in full expression (LIFE)?

With the exception of perhaps the clarity and intensity of the heavenly experience expressed by those who have had a NDE, is there anything that was described or experienced that is not fully available to us right here in this moment on this magnificent planet Earth? Is not unconditional love available to us when we let go of judgment? Is not indescribable beauty available to us when we fully immerse ourselves in the beauty that surrounds us and in fact, is inherent in us? Are not peace, joy and happiness available to us when we are released from the invisible chains of fear, worry and concern that bind us?

All we have to do is allow ourselves to have the experience, to actually be the experience. Have you ever been to the Grand Canyon or some other awe-inspiring place on Earth and literally had no words to describe what you were feeling? Have you ever experienced an incredible sunrise or sunset that literally swept you away? Have you ever been completely lost in any experience, whether it be love, laughter, joy, or happiness to the point you lost all sense of time, thought, or Self? There were no boundaries, no limits, no thoughts, no time, beginning or end.

Heaven on Earth is the integration of our Divine Spirit (Heaven) with our Human spirit (Earth). It is the fullest, most complete expression and experience of our Self and the Divine we can have while in human form. You are Heaven on Earth expressed and experienced.

Chapter 12

Principle of Non-Attachment

"Be ye as a passerby" is a statement attributed to Yeshua (Jesus). It means we are to experience all life has to offer while on Earth through the experience and expression of our Self without becoming attached to any of it. We are in this world but not of this world.

Another phrase, this from the literal translation of the Lord's Prayer from its original Aramaic by Dr. Rocco Errico, supports the invitation to be as a passerby:

"And you let us not enter into materialism.
But you separate us from error."

From this translation, we see it is our choice as to whether we "enter into materialism" that is, become attached to the things of this world. And "you separate us from error" means we are not who we think we are based on the error of our thinking, beliefs, judgments or mistakes. The translation of the Lord's Prayer from Aramaic by Dr. Rocco Errico can be read in its entirety at the conclusion of this book.

The principle of nonattachment tells us we are not to identify or label ourselves as anyone or anything. We are not what we do, nor are we who others say we are. In most cases, we are not who we believe ourselves to be. This is because who we believe ourselves to be is often attached to experiences, expectations and the limiting beliefs we hold about ourselves and others. These beliefs lead to judgment which cannot coexist with non-attachment. Furthermore, non-attachment is living without attachment to any ideologies or dogma that would take us away from our knowledge, experience, expression, and most importantly, trust in Self.

When I have spoken on this topic I have been told that it brings to mind an image of one going through life emotionless, unaffected, and uncaring. Just the opposite is true. For being a passerby is being fully engaged in life, fully invested in all that life is and has to offer. It is being deeply and passionately in love with life while living in full expression and experience of who one is and desires to be.

When we are attached to the things of this world we suffer when we no longer have the experience of them. This is not to say we shouldn't love deeply and have lifelong relationships, especially with our children, family, and friends. This doesn't mean we shouldn't enjoy the material aspects of life by living in a nice home or driving a nice car or that we shouldn't strive to be successful at something we enjoy. We might do something that makes us well known in the world but we are not what we did, the job or status we held or the relationships we were in. We are who and what had the experiences of these things. When the experience ends we still exist as the expression of the Divine that we were before the experience. We are here to live in non-attachment of the experiences created for the Divine to experience and express it Self through us.

To live life in full expression requires one to be as a passerby. We are not living in full expression if we are attached to thoughts and beliefs held by others about who they believe we are or should be. We are not living in full expression if we are attached to the outcomes of what we do or have done, our successes or perceived failures. We are not living in full expression if we are attached to labels we accept and identify that do not reflect our True Nature.

> *"It is when we experience life non-attached that we are free to experience it as it unfolds in each precious moment, in its perfection and glory as it is intended."*

Another important aspect of the principle of nonattachment is that we are to experience the full range of human emotions. It is when we suppress our emotions that we are resisting the flow of life. By allowing the full range of human emotions we are alive and engaged with life and therefore fully expressing and experiencing our Self. Non-attachment in this case means not becoming attached to the emotion beyond its expression. As an example, allow your Self to experience and express anger but do not become an angry person. Allow your Self to experience and express sorrow but do not become a sad or depressed person.

You might be thinking, well what about joy, love, and happiness? Aren't these emotions to which we would want to be attached? Here's the difference; you are these expressions. You are joy, love, and happiness. Living in full expression allows for the grandest experience of Self, which is joy, love, and happiness. You cannot detach from that which you are, however you can choose whether or not to express and experience it.

Be ye as a passerby. As you move through life, acknowledge all that is; appreciate all that is; experience all that is; and love all that is without being attached to any of it. In so doing you will experience life fully, wholly (holy) and freely as your True Self.

Just Let Go

A very common piece of advice given to folks who are frustrated, stressed out or just plain unhappy with everything, including themselves, is to just let go. Sounds simple, right? We all seem to have an idea of what it means, yet most struggle with actually doing it. What's the problem? Well, it seems that the problem is we really don't know what it means to let go and as a result, don't know how to let go.

Letting go is acceptance and allowance. Accepting where you are in life, accepting the experiences you are having in life, accepting who you are in this moment in life and accepting the truth that you have the power to change it. And then, allowing your Self to do so. Letting go is accepting and allowing without judgment. This isn't to imply that we just accept life as the cards we were dealt and therefore can do nothing about our life experiences. It means accepting, "OK, here I am. I take full responsibility for where I am and I take full responsibility for where I will go from this moment forward." Each moment presents the opportunity to change what is to what is desired, however to do so you must let go of any belief that says you have no say in how life unfolds. In an interesting paradoxical way, letting go is regaining personal power.

Letting go is releasing the white knuckle grip on all of those "things" you believe are causing your difficulty or misery and embracing all that life offers while trusting it is always for your highest and best. Letting go is the refocusing of your attention from what was and what you fear might be, to what is and can be. It is being present to now. Letting go is moving from resistance and attachment to flow. Give your Self permission to enjoy and embrace life fully and completely without attachment to any of it. Once again, be in this world not of this world.

A challenge to letting go is the thought that if we do all hell will break loose. And quite frankly, that is exactly what will happen and exactly what you want to happen. Once hell breaks loose you have the opportunity to be free of it, if you choose to.

"The hell you experience is the hell you so dearly hold on to."

Here are three keys to letting go and getting into flow with life.

1. Be aware of and vigilant with your thoughts and beliefs. Are they limiting or liberating? Are they holding you back or propelling you forward?
2. You always have a choice. No matter the circumstances there is always a choice that can be made, even if it is to do or not do something, this is still a choice with its attendant consequences. Make choices consistently in alignment with the experiences you desire.
3. Life is not static. The more we *attempt* to hold on to the way things are, the more challenging life becomes. The more we accept and allow the dynamic nature of life, the more enjoyable and fulfilling our experiences of life.

Chapter 13

Being Perfectly Human

At some point in my life I developed the belief that consciously walking a spiritual path meant I was to lead a perfect life, or at the very least, I was to be working toward this perfect life. The more aware I became of this belief the more I questioned where it came from. I don't recall being told or reading somewhere that I had to live life a certain way or be a certain way to consciously be on my spiritual path. I am not speaking of what one might have been told or believe through the teachings of their accepted religion. I am speaking from a pure spiritual perspective of how I believed one must live to be spiritual, especially when sharing spiritual concepts. Further contemplation led me to a question, the answer to which gave me peace with the life I am living. What is a perfect life?

I have to admit I struggled with this idea when I first started my conscious inner work. I thought I had to speak and behave in certain ways; otherwise I wouldn't be living in full expression; I wouldn't be living the spiritual life. This caused me stress because I felt as though I couldn't just flow with life. I felt constricted and concerned about how others might view me. I would get annoyed, frustrated or angry and question why I was feeling this way. After all I was living my life as I believed someone consciously walking a spiritual path should. I was not supposed to express or experience the same emotions or feelings that those not consciously on their path experienced.

What I realized was that subconsciously I was working hard to remove the human experience from life. I had taken on the belief that to be spiritual meant one didn't act or think as a human. The funny thing is that the harder I worked to live this so-called spiritual life the more the human side appeared. It finally dawned on me that living a spiritual life and following one's perceived chosen path is not about being a perfect human: it is being *perfectly human*. What I now know is that it is the integration and expression of our spiritual aspect with our human aspect that provides for the fullest life experience, and ultimately, the grandest experience and expression of Self.

"Life is not about being a perfect human;
it is being perfectly human."

We all incarnate the human body with the same fallibilities and vulnerabilities. The fact that the physical body is at all times subject to the possibility of pain and suffering is both the greatest challenge and greatest benefit to anyone who incarnates the physical body. There is the innate knowing that at any time any one of us can suffer physically and emotionally and that in some ways life on the Earth plane is never secure. And yet, it is in rising above this that we learn to claim our spiritual heritage and spiritual beingness.

Being perfectly human is about allowing and experiencing all that life is in every form it takes. It is being curious about life, in awe of life, respectful of life and knowing that every one of us are here to experience our Self within the vagaries of life. What I realized as I struggled to lead a spiritual life was that I am living my perfect life. In Truth, the life every Soul lives is the perfect life for the grandest experience and expression of that Soul during that souljourn, otherwise it wouldn't be living it. Our human experiences are perfectly created for the expansion, experience and expression of Self.

"Life always presents exactly what is needed when it is needed."

We have all heard that what we resist persists. The more I resisted what was being presented to me the more intense certain situations became. It finally got to the point when I almost had to accept what was being presented because of the intensity of the situation. Notice I said almost *had to accept*. There is always a choice in what we want to experience. We can choose to accept and have the experience of whatever is being presented or we can choose to resist and have the experience that resistance will bring. Neither choice is right or wrong; however, each choice brings with it a different experience of Self.

Resistance stems from a reluctance or unwillingness to accept change (life) as it is presented. Even though change is constant, it is the uncertainty of what that change looks like that elicits fear. When looking through the eyes of fear we are unable to see the benefit behind the change and therefore only see that which might be challenging or difficult. When we see challenge and difficulty our first response is usually resistance. We don't want to go there. We think to ourselves, life is hard enough as it is, and now this. When is it going to end? When will life finally give me a break?

Suffering is a choice. Suffering is our attachment to feelings, emotions, thoughts, and beliefs that no longer serve us. The truth is, we can easily choose to end suffering by releasing our Self from the attachment. Life consistently offers the opportunity to do so; however, it requires a letting go of that which we have held as true about our Self. When the conscious decision to no longer accept suffering is made, we free our Self to embrace and experience life fully as it is presented in the current moment.

Pay particular attention to any patterns that develop where you are presented similar life circumstances time and time again. When this occurs it is most likely your Soul saying this is an experience it desires to have and regardless of any resistance you might put forth you will have this experience. I (your soul) will continue to create opportunities for this experience until the conscious choice is made to allow the experience. Engaging your awareness at all times is vital. Being consciously aware of what is happening around and within you frees you to make choices that provide for the grandest experience and expression of Self.

Here are a few questions to consider that can change your perspective on life and therefore your experience of life.

1. What if instead of resisting life you are in flow with life?
2. What if you accepted that everything life presented, in whatever form it took, was for your benefit?
3. What if you viewed change through the eyes of potential – the greater expression and experience of Self– instead of through eyes of challenge, difficulty or instance of victimhood?
4. What if you accepted change as the natural process for your continuous experience and expression of Self, your very purpose for being here on the Earth plane?
5. What if you *consciously* created change for the grandest experience and expression of Self possible instead of waiting for change to take place?

6. How might knowing you are the creator of your life experiences bring peace to your life?

As you consider change and perhaps your resistance to or fear of change, what would you say if you were asked how you would like to experience life in three, five, or ten years? Would you like it be as it is now or do you desire it to be different? Most people say they want and expect life to be different from the way it is now. In fact, they would like it to be different. Perhaps better stated, they would like their experience of life and their experience of Self to be different from the way it is today.

Life moving forward is going to be different. Life is fluid. Life flows whether we are in flow with it or not just as water continues to flow over and around a boulder that would resist it. In the end however, it is the boulder that surrenders to the persistence of the water that would wear it away and reshape it. And so it is with us. We eventually surrender to the persistence of life and come to accept all it offers as it wears away all that would deny the experience and expression of our true Self. Surrender is not about giving up; it is giving in. It is giving in to the magnificence of what can be, the magnificence of all that we are, the magnificence of Self. Our boulders in life are the limiting thoughts and beliefs we hold about our Self.

Regardless of how much we resist what life is offering, life will eventually wear down our limiting beliefs, not causing us to throw our hands in the air in surrender but to raise our hands in victory as we accept that life always has and always will offer what we need for the grandest experience and expression of Self.

Change makes life dynamic, exciting and worth experiencing. Change brings benefit to life. Change brings energy to life; it brings life to life. Change is creation; therefore we are here to experience creation.

As the creator of our own life experiences, creation places the power of what can be within us.

"Change is not a choice; whether you embrace it or you resist it is."

Change will occur. However, if the change is as a result of our creation, our intention, then our life experiences will be those we desire and not those that show up by default. Change/creation is the opportunity to experience and express ourselves under ever evolving circumstances that deepen our knowledge, experience, and relationship with Self.

"When we are in concert with the song of life,
even though the melody changes, we still sing our song,
only now with grander expression."

Chapter 14

Why is This Happening to Me?

Have you ever considered how and why things happen in life as they do? Many believe there is a purpose behind everything that happens, yet struggle to comprehend a purpose behind a young child being stricken with cancer or the senseless murder of an innocent human being.

There is a dynamic invisible intelligence at play behind the scenes that is responsible for the orchestration of life's events and experiences. Each experience is for the "soul" purpose of living in full expression within the context of each event as we return to the truth of who we truly are. There is a magic and mystery to life that we do not, and cannot, fully comprehend from our human level of thinking and understanding. And yet, the answer to the question is quite simple, but incomplete. Incomplete because it doesn't address the human emotions and feelings that are more than a part of the experience, they are the experience.

The answer isn't intended to in any way minimize the impact of these experiences on our emotional, mental, physical and spiritual states. In fact, just the opposite is true. The answer illustrates the perfection behind the opportunities life presents to experience the richness of each human emotion as we live in full expression.

The simple answer is that things happen when they do because the conditions for them are perfect. Meaning that everything necessary for an event has come together to form a matrix from which the event evolves. What is not so simple to comprehend or conceive is the magnitude of all that comes together for an event to unfold. As an example, timing, in addition to being the point at which all has come together for an event to occur, has conditions attached to it as well. Timing isn't just as it relates to the main character for which an event unfolds, it is the perfect moment at which everything and everyone connected to the event can most benefit from the event.

Timing also takes into consideration our capacity to receive the experience of the event. We have all heard that we are not given something for which we are not prepared nor capable of handling. Isn't it interesting that when we observe someone else going through a difficult time we state that we could never do what they are doing? And yet, when we are personally going through a challenging experience we just do what we know we need to do. Yes, we might question if and how we can do it, but ultimately we rise to the occasion because we are capable of doing so. And in doing so, we gain a clearer understanding and experience of who we truly are.

Some might question the use of the words benefit or benefitted as they relate to challenging life events. It brings into question one's belief about the purpose of life itself. How this question is answered determines in great measure how life will unfold and be experienced by that individual. For me, the purpose of life is the full experience and expression of each Soul as it journeys through the labyrinth of life to its full understanding and experience of who and what it truly is. Every experience, although at times difficult to comprehend, offers the perfect circumstances for this full expression.

"Life is perfect despite evidence to the contrary."

On a Soul level we set specific intentions that can be met by the events that life presents, most of which we call to our Self specifically for that purpose. Additionally, we each play a role in the life experiences of others for the "Soul" purpose of these intentions being fulfilled while living in full experience and expression of who we are.

Life is difficult, yet it yields perfectly the experiences best suited for regaining the truth of who we are. Observe what life is presenting without judgment, anger or fear, knowing that it would not have been presented if it was not perfect for all concerned.

Have I Done Something Wrong?

Have I done something wrong? Am I a bad person? Did I do something in a previous life for which I am now paying the price? The simple truth is, "No." You have done nothing wrong. You are not a bad person, and no you are not paying for something you might have done in a previous life.

The answers to these questions were given to me as my son was going through the very difficult experience of losing his beloved dog, Kierra who was hit by car. It was one of the most heart-breaking experiencing I have witnessed and been a part of, and yet, it is life unfolding in its perfection.

My son, trying to make sense of why Kierra was taken from him started to question if it was his fault as a result of choices he made and who he was being. Not knowing how to respond I opened my heart and asked for the words to express what I was feeling and what I know to be the truth. This is what I received and shared with my son.

"Life is difficult and in its difficulty is its perfection. Every experience we have individually and collectively is for the benefit of knowing and experiencing our Self fully and completely within the context of each experience.

When we have a difficult experience, like the loss of your beloved Kierra, this is not Life telling you that you have been bad and need to be punished. It is not Life telling you that you are not a good person. It is Life offering you the opportunity to look at your life, to look at your Self and open yourself to all that Life has to offer.

When something difficult happens in life it does not happen to us, it happens for us. Yes, the appearance is that it happens to a person because they are the one more directly impacted by what takes place. However, it offers everyone who is impacted the opportunity to look at themselves, to assess who they are, where they are, what they are doing, and how they are relating to Life and all that it offers.

What happens when there is a tragedy? Of course there is the emotional pain that is experienced and felt, but there is also the outpouring of love and compassion towards us from those around us. It is their relating to the experience that we are going through because they too have had the experience in their own way. It also allows us to assess if we are compassionate towards others. When a friend or family member, or even a stranger, is having a difficult time, do I express my compassion for them and what they are going through? And if you don't or haven't, it doesn't make you a bad person. It just means that you haven't allowed your heart to be cracked open and vulnerable to the truth and beauty of who you truly are.

Whenever we have thoughts of, "Am I being punished? Am I a bad person?", it is your Soul asking you to bring into question who you are being. Am I being kind and loving to all others, am I being non-judgmental, am I being true to whom I know my Self to be?

These events, like Kierra passing, are painful and yet they can also be the most beneficial in life. This isn't to imply that Kierra's life was taken for your benefit. Random events like this take place all of the time. But in these random events lies the very specific opportunity to make changes in how we perceive life, how we perceive our Self, how we live life and how we express who we are in relation to Life.

Complete strangers found you on the side of the road hovering over Kiera's lifeless body. They demonstrated tremendous compassion and love towards you and Kierra. They didn't have to, but they did. The feelings you have experienced as a result of this show of love and compassion are the same feelings others experience when you extend yourself and express love and compassion towards them.

Everything is energy vibrating at different frequencies. The lower frequencies are fear, hate, anger, frustration, sadness, depression, doubt etc. When we are in this lower frequency, which we all are from time to time, we draw to ourselves more low frequency experiences that perpetuate the lower frequency experience. When we are in and operate from the higher frequencies of love, joy, happiness and compassion we attract experiences that allow for more of these experiences.

We are intended to have the experience of grief, sadness, frustration, anger, etc., however we are not intended to stay in that frequency. The key is being aware of when we are in those lower frequencies and making the conscious choice to lift our Self out of them to the higher frequencies.

Love, joy, happiness and compassion are our intrinsic means of expressing who we truly are. The reason we have such a strong desire for these expressions is because we have a strong desire to live in full expression of that truth, and when we do not, we allow ourselves to fall into the lower frequencies where we question who we are, and if we are actually worthy of those higher frequency experiences of love, joy, happiness and compassion.

Kierra died doing what Kierra loved to do…run wild and free, exploring, sniffing, chasing and being the expression of love, joy and happiness that she was. Dogs like Kierra provide the greatest example of these expressions for us stubborn humans. She was always happy, always wagging her tail, always willing and ready to play and express her love for you. She always expressed her gratitude for all that you provided her by licking, kissing and cuddling with you. She never complained. She might have whined on occasion but that was because she knew she could get you to give her the attention she wanted if she did! She accepted everything that happened in her life. She didn't hold grudges when you reprimanded her for something she might have done, which in every case was nothing more than doing what dogs do. She was always forgiving and ready to move onto the next adventure with you and of course her sweet sister, Morgan.

She knew that by demonstrating love toward you (and others) she would always receive love in return. She didn't judge those around her as being unworthy of her love, she loved freely because it was/is who she is. Through Kierra's living you have been given the blessing of her love and companionship. Through her passing you have been given an experience of the depths of your own capacity to love and you have received an experience of the depth and capacity for love and compassion that others have for you.

Kierra, through her passing, is inviting you to look at your life, not because you have done something wrong or are a bad person… but because you have so much more to give and receive if you would just allow it to be so. My heart broke wide open when I answered your phone call and heard and felt the pain you were experiencing. Words will never express how much I love you…I just trust that you know."

Chapter 15

Eyes of Potential

A few years ago while attending a business conference I was called on stage to be recognized for some recent success. While on stage I was handed the microphone and asked to share a few inspiring words that might be of benefit to those in the audience. Anyone who knows me knows I am not one to shy away from a microphone, however on this particular occasion I was caught off guard. There I stood looking out at the gaze of the expectant audience with nothing close to an inspirational thought coming to mind. I am sure the silence lasted for no more than 5 or 10 seconds. However at the time it seemed like an eternity. Suddenly my mind came to rest on a topic that had come to my awareness during one of my morning walks. I had not explored it much and certainly was not prepared to present it to a live audience. Yet I gave into the moment and spoke about a condition we all suffer from at one time or another: *fearsightedness.*

So what is this condition called fearsightedness? Unlike nearsightedness, a condition of the eye usually corrected by corrective lenses or glasses, fearsightedness is a condition of the mind that causes one to view life as always difficult, challenging, fearful, and full of obstacles. No matter where someone suffering from fearsightedness might look, everything is colored by their fear of what they believe might happen (usually a worst-case scenario) regardless of any decision or action they take.

We all know or have met people who view life in this way. They are not easy to be around and are the type that can walk outside on a gorgeous sunny day and instead of enjoying and appreciating the beauty of the day will say, "yeah but it's raining somewhere." Fearsightedness robs us of our personal power. Imagine your life filled with constant worry about potential difficulties or tragedy, or events from the past without any thought being given to the possibility that something wonderful or positive could happen. This is always looking for the proverbial second shoe to drop. A favorite quote of mine about life is by French philosopher Michel de Montaigne.

"My life has been full of many terrible misfortunes, most of which never happened."

This sums up what those suffering from fearsightedness experience. The vast majority of those "terrible misfortunes" never come to pass, and yet, because of the amount of energy and emotion put toward those fears they have an experience of them as if they are actually taking place. And in some cases the amount of energy and emotion placed toward the fears is sufficient enough to attract those circumstances into their lived experience. This of course then supports their belief that life is fearful because "these bad things continue to happen to me."

Worry and concern take us out of the present moment and blind us to what life is offering. Being out of the present moment we are not available or receptive to the goodness and beauty of life. Imagine how much of the goodness of life is missed when life is viewed through the eyes of fearsightedness. Imagine the limited experience and expression of one's Self if their focus is always on what might happen to them or around them instead of what they might create that fosters joy, love and happiness.

In the most extreme cases of fearsightedness people believe and therefore experience life as being against them. They believe that whatever life presents is yet another attempt to prevent them from receiving and experiencing the goodness of life. They are resigned to the belief that it doesn't matter what choices they make or actions they take because life has its own agenda. And that agenda is usually something working against them to prevent the experience of life they truly desire, a life of joy, happiness, peace, love and beauty.

A fearsighted view centers on the fear of uncertainty even though uncertainty contains the possibility of something magnificent. Uncertainty is nothing more than not knowing a specific outcome. In and of itself uncertainty is not difficult, challenging or fearful; however our thoughts can make it so. Looking at uncertainty from a neutral perspective, no thoughts or emotions attached, there is at least a fifty-fifty chance that something favorable will result. And the percentage always increases in favor of the belief that is held and the choices and actions taken. The point is that the more we place our focus on the fearful outcome the more likely we are to have that experience. Conversely, when we step into uncertainty with the expectation that it will result in an incredible, magnificent experience the more likely we are to create and enjoy that experience.

Defending Our Misery

Are you serious, defending your misery at the expense of happiness? Who would do that? Why would someone do that? Yes, I am serious and I think you will see why and how as we continue this discussion. Let's first look at what is meant by misery. An official definition of misery according to the Merriam-Webster dictionary is: *a state of great unhappiness and emotional distress.* We often associate misery with physical pain and long-term discomfort. However within the context of this topic, misery is in reference to unhappiness and emotional distress.

When asked what one wants most out of life, a common response is, "I just want to be happy." Does this mean that most folks are unhappy or that they believe they could be happier? And if they are unhappy, and they know it, why don't they do something to change? What is preventing happiness in the first place? And misery, why would I defend my misery? Why would I fight to be unhappy? Why would I deny myself the experience of life that I desire?

Misery results from the sameness, the mundane of everyday life, the feeling of being stuck with things as they are with no way out. It is the belief we have to do things out of obligation or responsibility and therefore put the experiences we truly desire on the so-called backburner. Yes, there are things to which we have made a commitment like supporting our family, showing up at work each day, paying our bills, etc., but these are not the limit of who we are and what we have available to us.

The primary cause of misery is Self-denial. An unwillingness to take responsibility for our lives and allow for the full experience and expression of who we truly are that is persistent in its desire to be expressed. Life is limitless in what it offers as our experience. We are always at a point of choice where we choose how we will experience life, even when it comes to choosing happiness over misery; regardless of the circumstances in which we find ourselves. Henry David Thoreau summed it up beautifully in his quote:

"Most men lead lives of quiet desperation and go to the grave with the song still in them."

Your song is the expression of your true Self in whatever form you choose. What is the song within you that is waiting to be sung? What are you inspired to do or be that you know would bring you an experience of joy and happiness but for "your" reasons you have not given yourself permission to choose?

Ask yourself why you have not given yourself permission. The answers to this question will help identify the ways in which you are defending your misery at the expense of your happiness.

Some examples might be:

- **I can't because**......Fill in the blank. How you complete this statement is a defense of your misery.
- **Remaining where I am is easier or more convenient** than what I "believe" is necessary to move on. And yet, all we need to do is choose to allow the experience of what we desire to experience.
- **Blaming other people or events** for where you are in life instead of taking responsibility. It is only when we take responsibility for our life experiences that we can change them.
- **Worry and concern**. Allowing fear over what might happen or has happened to take precedence over what we can create and experience that is in alignment with our Self-expression and desire for happiness.
- **Not worthy**. Living from the belief that this is the life I have been given, there is nothing I can do to change it. Others much more deserving than me have the opportunity for happiness but not me.

- **Being afraid of what might be lost** in the process instead of excited, joyful and motivated about what will be gained. We never lose anything that is in alignment with and beneficial to whom we are and are in the process of becoming and experiencing.
- **Fear of losing the happiness** once we gain it. Every time I gain something it is taken away from me. Understand that happiness is a state of being in this world and is not dependent on anything, any person, or any event. Happiness is our full expression, understanding and relationship with our Self and the Divine.
- **Uncertainty.** Fear of the unknown. We become comfortable with the known and therefore are more willing to remain in our misery even though the unknown holds the potential for our greatest experiences and expression of who we truly are.

These limiting thoughts and beliefs act as blinders offering a very limited view of the potential that life offers. These statements made to our Self, mostly subconsciously, are nothing more than excuses for not taking responsibility for one's life experiences. Nothing could be further from the truth. We are responsible for our life experiences. Our outward experiences of life are a reflection of our inward thoughts, beliefs, and feelings. Put more succinctly: they are a reflection of our relationship with our Self; how and what we think, believe and feel about our Self.

How do we move out of a life of quiet discontent or misery into a life of happiness, joy and full expression? By,

- **Simply choosing to**…
- **Trusting our inspiration/intuition, our Self**.

- **Knowing your song** and the "why" for having the desire to sing it.
- **Knowing you have nothing to lose** by doing so other than the misery within which you have chosen to live.
- **Knowing that Life, the Universe, doesn't want you to live in misery**. However, it is compelled to support you in whatever choices you make. Choose consciously and wisely.

When we take the time to question and explore what we believe, why we believe it and why we make the decisions we do, we make better and more empowering decisions. By questioning what and why we believe what we believe we can change our perspective from what we can't do to what we are capable of doing. With this new perspective we are more likely to make decisions that move us in the direction of the experiences we desire rather than experiences we fear.

By questioning your thoughts and beliefs you are doing so to make certain you are operating from *your* truth as you know it in the moment, that you are not doubting. To doubt is to distrust or be uncertain about what you know and hold as true. When we question our thoughts and beliefs we are looking for clarity. We dig deeper for greater understanding and meaning. In doing so, we reveal and create the opportunity to let go of thoughts and beliefs that no longer serve us. We open our Self to new beliefs that empower and support us. We embrace and trust that which we come to know as true, not because someone else has said so, but because it is what we believe and hold as true about our Self in the moment. All of this is so we can better experience and express our Self as fully and completely as we can.

When we doubt our Self we have lost faith. We are no longer, if we ever were, trusting in our Self, trusting in the Universe and the goodness of life. We are not honoring and respecting our Self for who we are and for what we are capable. This is especially true where other people are concerned. We accept other's opinions over our own placing more value on what they think about us than on what we believe and know about our Self. This doesn't mean what they say or think about us is not true or valid or that we can't agree with them. We can agree with them; however, we agree because we know it to be true and therefore base our belief on our truth and not the opinion of someone else.

By now you might be wondering what any of this has to do with my standing on stage without knowing what I was going to share. Here's my point. If I had succumbed to fearsightedness I would not have spoken as I did. I would not have demonstrated that I had something of value to share or that I trusted what I had to share. I would not have gained more confidence and trust in myself to speak extemporaneously. I would have denied myself and everyone in attendance the experience of my Self-expression. I don't know if what I shared had an impact on anyone in the audience. What I do know is that it had an impact on me, not so much in terms of what I said as in the fact that I trusted and honored my Self by speaking as I did.

Fearsightedness is corrected through clear-sightedness whereby we are aware, consciously aware, of who we are and of what we are capable of creating and experiencing. We are more trusting and respectful of our Self, more trusting in the goodness of life. We know that the Universe, God wants us to live a life of joy, peace, love, happiness and overall well-being. With clear-sightedness we see life through eyes of possibility and potential, not fear or limitation.

How different might life be if we moved from the fear of what we think might happen to the potential of what we can make happen? By correcting fearsightedness through the corrective lens of possibility and potential we free our Self to more fully experience and express who we are while receiving all that life has to offer.

"It is unfortunate that we are too often fearful of what might happen instead of emboldened by what we might create."

The Deconstruction of Fear

Most have heard or read the definition of fear as it is expressed through the acronym of its letters, False Evidence Appearing Real. Some might have heard or read of another lesser known, more tongue in cheek, acronym; Forget Everything and Run! While both of these give a perspective on fear, neither gets to the truth of fear, which is that it is an illusion that controls many of our decisions and subsequently our life experiences.

Fear as I am describing it here is not the fear associated with imminent danger in any given moment, but the fear we associate with what has already happened or what we "fear" might happen. Fear that we associate with imminent danger is actually quite interesting in that in the moment we are not actually fearful but in a heightened state of awareness, and therefore, more acutely alert to what is happening around us. In this heightened state of awareness, we are fully present to the moment.

Fear is a construct of the mind. It doesn't exist anywhere but within the mind and yet we experience the effects of it within the physical body. It has nothing to do with imminent danger but everything to do with choices we make, actions we take, and ultimately the life we experience. We have all had experiences when we felt fearful about something we wanted to do, even when the desire to do so was strong. And unfortunately, because of this fear we chose not to take action and move forward on this desire.

How many times have you awakened in the morning with a great idea or inspiration but by lunch you talked yourself out of it? Why? How is it that in the morning you had what you felt was a "can't miss" inspiration and then slowly allowed the fear of what others might say, what others might think, what others might do...blah, blah, blah... keep you from expressing in the world this inspiration you were given?

Since fear is a construct of the mind it can be deconstructed with the use of these four tools of personal empowerment. And as you will read, fear can be deconstructed by fear itself.

Four Tools of Personal Empowerment

Fearlessness. Your first thought might be that if you lived fearlessly then you wouldn't experience fear and there would be nothing to deconstruct. And while this is true, it takes being bold and courageous in the face of that *perceived* fear to live fearlessly. It means stepping across the threshold of certainty into the unknown with the joyous anticipation that what you desire to experience is what will result.

To live fearlessly you must fear less. You must understand the nature of fear and recognize that most of what you fear has no substance or validity. You must have faith that whatever you have been inspired to create and experience is intended, and therefore, will be fully supported as you bring that inspiration to life.

Living fearlessly is not only fully trusting oneself, but Life itself.

"Living fearlessly is knowing that no matter what happens, it happens for you not to you."

Engage. Fully engage in life. Take action despite the feelings of fear you might have. Nothing disperses fear like action taken towards the experiences you desire. Nothing creates momentum like fully engaging in the creation process by making *conscious choices* in alignment with the life you desire.

As you engage in Life you expand your experience of Self and therefore your personal power. The more you experience your personal power the more you realize how powerful you truly are. The impacts we *allow* fear to have on our life are in direct proportion to the degree to which exercise and experience our personal power.

Awareness. Be aware of the limits you have placed on yourself through your perceived fears. Recognize the opportunities that are and have always been available to you but were not seen due to the blindness imposed by fear. Declare that *Enough Is Enough* and that you will no longer subordinate your personal power to fear. Make choices out of your enhanced awareness that lessen or eliminate the impact of fear and lead to the experiences you desire.

Fear is deconstructed by your awareness of it, feeling it, acknowledging it and owning it as something you created and continue to hold on to. Allow Life to flow without resistance (fear) and you will experience it as it was intended for your greatest experience and expression of Self.

Release. Let go of any attachments to thoughts or beliefs you hold of your Self and life that in any way limit your fullest experience and expression of your Self and life. Fear results from placing more value on the opinion of the "world" than you place on your own. When we place more value on the opinion of the world we are in constant fear of not living up to that opinion. And in Truth, the only opinion that matters is yours.

Release any attachments to the outcome, especially those that are less than what you are capable of creating and experiencing. Release any attachment to the way you think Life should be. Allow and embrace the beauty and perfection of the way Life is. Release any attachment to who you believe you are. Live in authenticity. Authenticity is living from the core and depth of your being. It is living in truth and transparency. When you are transparent, and therefore living in truth, there is nothing to fear.

Fear is actually an ally. It stands as a doorway to our greater understanding and experience of our Self and higher consciousness. All we have to do is fearlessly cross the threshold.

Chapter 16

Magnificence

We prevent the full experience and expression of Self due to limiting beliefs—those so-called truths we hold about ourselves. And yet, if we acknowledge and appreciate our accomplishments we would readily see the overwhelming evidence that we are having a much greater impact on our own life as well as the lives of others. We would accept our limiting beliefs as nothing more than illusions causing them to return to the nothingness from which they came.

A client told me that she didn't believe she had accomplished anything significant or meaningful to this point in her life. Because of our work together I knew about some of her past. In fact, many things that she had done were significant; however, they were not significant in the way she believed she needed them to be.

The first question I asked was if her two sons were happy and healthy. She answered, "Yes, they are." I asked her if she had provided them with a good life, giving them all she could, including the love only a mother can provide. Again she answered, "Yes."

She had worked two jobs in order to bring in enough money for the family to enjoy a comfortable life. She would finish one job at 5:00 p.m. and drive to the second which was a retail store where she would work until 10:00 p.m., many nights without stopping for dinner. I asked if working the two jobs benefitted her family. She answered, "Yes."

There are many more examples of what she experienced and the significance of who she is and what she has accomplished. While these might seem like simple things, they are important to those who receive direct benefit from what she has done and who she is. More importantly, they are integral to her expression and experience of Self.

Do you think my client's children think that what their mom has done is insignificant? Do you think that who she is and has demonstrated herself to be will leave an imprint on her boys and who they become and how they relate to the world?

This client held an illusion, a limiting belief, of who she was, what she was capable of doing, and of what she had already accomplished. Her limiting beliefs obscured her knowing and acknowledging her true Self, even though it was her true Self that was being expressed.

This client now armed with an expanding awareness of her Self is stepping into uncertainty (possibility) with the knowing she is capable of moving beyond life's challenging opportunities. She knows that what she has to offer and who she is meaningful and relevant.

"The veil of limiting beliefs is pierced with our acknowledgement and appreciation of who we are and what we have accomplished, regardless of the scope or size of what was achieved."

Too often we judge ourselves against the life path of another. However, each life path is unique to the Soul that has chosen that life. Each life provides exactly what that Soul needs to live in full expression and experience of Self, otherwise that particular path would not have been chosen. Each person's contribution to humanity lies in each living his or her respective life in full expression of who he or she truly is.

Many years ago after a presentation, I noticed a woman making her way through the gathering of people in front of me. As I turned and our eyes met she said, "I heard you speak two years ago and what you said saved my daughter's life." With that she turned and walked away.

To this day I do not know who she was or what I said that could have possibly impacted her daughter in such a way. What I do know and learned from this experience is that I, all of us, have a far greater impact on the lives of others than we realize. I also became more aware of the impact others have on my life. When this woman told me that I had somehow made a difference she provided me with the inspiration to continue doing and being who I am, however with greater understanding and purpose.

I can easily succumb to the limiting belief that what I have to say has no meaning or value to others, or I can choose to believe that someone somewhere will find meaning or value. I choose the latter. I don't know who will be in the audience on any given day or who I will come across in normal day-to-day interactions. And most assuredly, I don't know how what I might say or do will impact them.

This knowing is one of the driving forces behind the writing of this book. I don't know who will pick it up and read it. I don't know how it will impact or influence those who do. I don't know if it will impact anyone for that matter, with the exception of one. That person is me. The writing of this book is my living in full expression and experiencing my Self in the role of an author.

What I do know is that if it had not been written it would have no influence or impact on anyone other than me. I would be living with a sense of wonder and perhaps regret. I would wonder what might have been if I had written the book. I would wonder what impact it might have had on the lives of others. I would wonder what impact it might have had on me and my life.

This book is in your hands because I chose to step into the uncertainty of what writing the book could bring rather than remain in the certainty of not writing it. This gets to the heart of living in full expression.

"When you are inspired to do something, whatever it is in you that calls to be expressed, answer the call. Be bold; cross the threshold into uncertainty with the joyous anticipation that you are in fact stepping into your magnificence, and that whatever results will benefit you and others, otherwise you would not have been inspired in the first place."

Stepping into Magnificence

With the exception of a few paragraphs that follow I am eliminating the phrase *stepping into uncertainty* because of the fear of the unknown it elicits for so many. Instead I invite you to think, feel, and speak from the knowing that you are always *stepping into your magnificence.* Stepping into magnificence is a more positive, more powerful, more truthful expression of who you are and what you desire to experience.

Why do we default to limiting beliefs when we have experiences that prove otherwise? Why don't we default to the truth that we are good enough and deserving enough to experience whatever we desire? Why not default to our magnificence?

A possible explanation is that we are more afraid of what we might lose than of what we might gain. The very thought that we might lose more than we gain is a limiting belief. We won't move toward what we truly desire if we fear or believe we will lose what we have in the process. This despite overwhelming evidence that when we have stepped into our magnificence we gained much more than we believed possible and left behind only that which no longer served us. And if nothing else, we always gain the experience of our Self as bold and courageous.

Think how different your life could be if instead of fearing what you might lose you were excited and curious about the unlimited potential of what might be gained. Imagine what might be gained if you stepped into your magnificence with the belief that something beneficial and wondrous would happen. This requires a letting go of the idea that uncertainty only pertains to negative or challenging situations and experiences. Letting go opens the door for anything and everything to happen, especially the experiences that would benefit us.

The key lies in our intention. If our intention as we step into our magnificence is that we *will* experience what we consider good and beneficial, then we will. It might not be in the form of what we thought it would be but it will absolutely be to our benefit.

"Stepping into our magnificence is crossing the border into the world of possibility and unlimited potential of what is and can be."

Stepping into our magnificence gives notice to the Universe that we are willing to follow the inspiration we are given. When we boldly follow that inspiration the Universe responds accordingly, because that is what the Universe is compelled to do.Another explanation for why we default to a limiting belief is that *we become too comfortable in our discomfort.* We believe, "even though things aren't exactly how I want them to be, they're not too bad. In fact, they could be much worse."

Becoming too comfortable in our discomfort is another way of saying we are unwilling to do or be what will bring us what we desire. We settle for the way things are, believing this is what life has to offer and there is nothing we can do to change it.

Nothing could be further from the truth. Life always presents that for which we believe we are worthy. Yes, it will take effort, conscious effort; however, when we are moving toward what we desire to experience the effort is not difficult; it is empowering. Once empowered, everything is possible. Challenges we encounter along the way are the opportunities we create to experience life and Self more fully.

"When we become too comfortable in our discomfort we deny our Self and the world the gift of our magnificence."

Let's play with an idea for a few minutes. After all, life is about creating, playing, and expanding. Imagine that you are standing on the rear deck of your home looking out over your backyard where you have planted beautiful trees, shrubs, and flowers. Within the backyard you feel safe and secure because you can see all that you created contained by the fence that surrounds it. But as you look beyond your fence you see an unlimited expanse of land that begs to be cultivated with beautiful gardens—much like what you have created within your backyard. You begin to wonder what it would be like to hop over the fence and create something new, something grander.

In your initial moment of inspiration, you know without a doubt that you can create something beautiful; something meaningful in that unlimited expanse of land that holds pure potential. And then you start to question yourself. Why do I need to move beyond the safety of my fenced-in yard? After all, I have a beautiful yard. And besides, what would others say if I were to expand beyond what I currently have? Who am I to have more of the potential of what life has to offer?

What makes me think I am worthy of more than others have? I know I have created this beautiful backyard but I am not good enough or talented enough to create something more expansive than what I am experiencing. And besides, if my yard is bigger then I will have more responsibility.

Stepping into magnificence is overwhelming and immobilizing to many. The vastness of what lies beyond the fence is more than can be handled. We settle into the comfort of a belief that it would be much easier and much safer to remain who we think we are than to expand into the magnificence of who we truly are.

What if instead of looking at unlimited potential in its totality we moved our fence back just a little? What if we incorporated a little more land within our backyard in which we could plant our flowers, trees, and shrubs? Instead of jumping over the fence and completely getting out of what we call our comfort zone, what if we expand it to include more of what we desire to experience?

This exercise isn't suggested to limit our view of who we can be by moving our fence back just a little. There will be some who will hop over the fence and run joyfully through the fields of potential creating everything and anything they have ever desired. Instead, it is intended to encourage those who feel overwhelmed by what lies beyond the safety and certainty of their backyard to take the initial steps into their magnificence and the unlimited field of potential and goodness life has to offer.

Stepping into our magnificence is the desire and willingness to courageously move beyond having become too comfortable in our discomfort to fully trusting the process of life and our Self. It is the knowing that when we take that joyous leap of faith all is provided for what we desire to create and experience.

Step into your magnificence with the expectation of the goodness life has to offer. Look at life with wonder, awe and curiosity. Be a conscious example, a courageous example, of what can be when one is freed from the disempowering illusions that are held. Expand your awareness to all that is happening around you and within you and know that it is all happening for you.

"When we step into our magnificence we gain knowledge, clarity, confidence, empowerment, an awareness of the great wisdom that lies within, and an opportunity for the full expression of that wisdom."

Chapter 17

It's All About Me

"It's all about me!" Say it again, this time out loud. How does that feel? What sensations do you experience in your body? Do you feel conflicted? Perhaps there is some resistance around the statement? Or do you feel a sense of freedom and empowerment?

Haven't we been taught that when we say or think, "It's all about me," we are selfish, arrogant, or self-centered? Haven't we been taught that we are our brother's keeper? Haven't we been taught we are responsible for one another and should do everything we can to benefit our fellow man?

There is no responsibility other than the one we have toward our Self to fully experience, express and be who we are. This is not a suggestion that we are to ignore our fellow man that is in need. At our core we are all beneficent beings. If our fellow man is in need we have an opportunity, a choice not an obligation, to be supportive or not. It is not out of any sense of obligation that we would choose to lend support but out of love toward our fellow man. It is not because of any karmic reward we think we might receive or fear of any karmic retribution. It is not because we believe we will be given a place in heaven or God will shine more favorably upon us. We extend our Self to others because it is the thing to do; it is who we are when we live from our core essence. It is what our Soul desires to be, express and experience.

We are not here to help everyone just as those whom we consider to be spiritual teachers and leaders did not help everyone. They recognized each of us has a path upon which we have chosen to walk and they discerned when it was appropriate to intercede. *Discernment is the key.* As we expand our knowledge and experience of Self we are more discerning in when, where, and to whom we extend our Self in support. However, when we consciously choose not to intercede on behalf of another we still benefit them by honoring their chosen path and allowing them the experience of Self they have chosen.

When we take responsibility for our own life and live in full expression of the truth of who we are, we will extend our Self toward others because it offers one of the grandest experiences and expressions of our Self we can have. And because, on a very deep level we know that serving one serves all.

The greatest relationship we can explore and experience, the relationship we are here to explore and experience, is our relationship with Self. It is in exploring and experiencing our relationship with Self that we become more capable of having a true relationship with others. Some may say the greatest relationship we are here to explore and experience is our relationship to and with God. It is my belief that our relationship with our Self is in fact the greatest expression and experience of God that can be. It is when we are in full expression that we most glorify that which I know as God.

Yes, we are responsible for our children as they grow and learn and become adults themselves. However, our responsibility lies more in the responsibility we take for our own lives therefore becoming a demonstration of how a responsible human being experiences and expresses their Self. It is a proven fact that children are more likely to become what they observe than what they are told. The more we are who we truly are, the more beneficial we are to others. The more we take responsibility for our life—our choices, thoughts, words, and deeds—the more we demonstrate to others who they are and of what they too are capable.

Most are probably familiar with the proverb, "Give a man a fish and you feed him for a day; teach a man to fish and you feed him for a lifetime." We can do things for others that might benefit them for a day, a week, or a month, however each one of us is ultimately responsible for our Self. This is no different than what every historical figure that we look upon as a spiritual teacher or mentor did. They were not incarnated to tell us what to do; they were here to show us who we are and why we are here.

Why Are We Here?

How do you answer this question? What thoughts come to mind when you consider the very purpose behind life? Do you believe this is a onetime event (lifetime) at which we get just one shot and then it's over? Or do you believe we have multiple lifetimes in which to experience and express our Self in the grandest ways possible?

Consider this. Wherever you are as you read this, or better yet, wherever it was that you were born, why do you believe you were born there? Of all of the places on this amazing planet where you could have been born, why do you believe you were born where you were and under your particular life circumstances? Take a few minutes and consider this, especially if you have never done so before. It is a very thought-provoking question that might open the way to a better understanding of why we are here.

If you believe that that which you call God or the Universe is non-judgmental, loves unconditionally, and intends for all to be happy, healthy and well, why would some people be born into the harshest of life conditions and others into conditions more favorable? This implies some are more deserving (judgment) of the more pleasing life experience while others (judged) less deserving and therefore born into harsher life conditions. If unconditional love towards all is an attribute of the Divine, how then does the Divine determine who is born where and under what conditions? Unconditional love means to love fully, completely, without judgment, and without conditions of any kind. Unconditional love does not contain within it the possibility of judgment.

So what is the answer? Why are some born into what we consider privileged circumstances and others unprivileged? We choose for ourselves, as an expression of the Divine, what it is we desire to experience in any given lifetime. It is from our choices that we are presented life circumstances perfectly created for the experiences we desire to have. The life experiences we desire are those we choose that facilitate our continuous spiritual growth, expansion, experience and expression of Self.

Chapter 18

This Time Around

As you might imagine, the title of this chapter implies that we have been here before and more than likely will be here again. The decision to come here to Earth is a joyful, conscious choice made prior to incarnation because of the rich, wide variety of experiences the Earth plane provides. If you believe we are here to explore, experience and express our Self in as many ways as possible through as many personalities as possible, then the concept of a singular life experience makes no sense. How would we explain the life of a child that dies young or a Soul born into a physically challenged body? Why would that child or Soul be given a limited opportunity in which to experience life or to experience and express his or her Self?

The most common answer I am given to these questions is that it is God's Will. I question why God would will for some Souls to experience more difficult, challenging life experiences than others. Why would God will a limited lifetime for one versus another? What would be the criteria against which God would make these decisions? This would be judgment—the judgment that one Soul deserves a more favorable life experience than another. The Divine is nonjudgmental.

We are born into circumstances that are perfectly created for the experiences we have *chosen* to have during this and subsequent soul-journs. We have multiple lifetimes that provide the opportunity for different life experiences and expressions under all life conditions and circumstances.

What is This Thing We Call Our Soul?

What is it that incarnates in the Earth plane in the human body to have these multiple life experiences? What is it that animates the human body so that it is alive and expressive? There are many descriptions and definitions of the Soul throughout history in different texts; however, the definition I accept and embrace is as follows.

"In esoteric terms the Soul is that part of you which has existed since the beginning of time as an aspect of GOD that experiences many different personalities in many different lifetimes. Even though the Soul will have this wide range of experiences, the core of the Soul Self is never dissipated, in truth it is enhanced. Ultimately, the Soul is Divine Light and Divine Love."

I think this is a beautiful description of the Soul. It was given to me by a dear friend and mentor, Christen McCormack, founder of the Spirit School of the Intuitive Arts. I find comfort in knowing that at my core I have always existed and always will and am in Truth, Divine Light and Divine Love.

When we think of God, Spirit, the Universe or the Divine, we usually associate it with or as unconditional love. If we consider ourselves an extension or aspect of the Divine as described, then we too must be unconditional love. When we consider our Soul an aspect of the Divine and therefore unconditional love we see the Truth of what and who we are contained within the letters of the word SOUL.

*"**S**ource **O**f **U**nconditional **L**ove."*

Your Soul at its very core—everybody's Soul at its core—is everything we have ever needed and has everything that we have ever needed, and yet it continues to seek more. This seeking is not a needy, grasping kind of seeking; it is a seeking that comes through the natural inclination of light (Divinity/Soul), which is to continuously expand upon itself. This expansion is a higher knowing, experience, and expression of itself through each one of us in each incarnation we have.

This time around is a reference to this specific phase of our experiences, expressions and expansion on Earth—a lifetime, which I refer to as a souljourn. In defining a souljourn as a temporary stay, the question might arise as to how a lifetime is considered a short stay when the average life expectancy is between seventy-five to eighty years. It is only from our Earth perspective that this seems like an extended period of time. In the spirit realm from which we emerge and return, each souljourn is but a moment in the infinite.

When we consider a souljourn with the above definitions in mind we understand that it is an opportunity for the Soul, through the experiences the Earth plane provides, to continuously expand upon, know, express, and experience itself more fully. Everywhere we look in life there is beauty even within our perceived difficulties, failures, or imperfections. There is beauty not only in the sense of the natural beauty we see and experience in nature and in one another but the beauty inherent in the perfection of the Divine design that is played out through each one of us.

Souljourns, as we all know through our personal life experiences can at times be difficult. We are confronted with situations that challenge us in many ways, and yet it is during these difficult times (challenging opportunities) that we can choose to experience and express more fully who we are and who we are in the process of being. It is our response to these challenging opportunities that reflects who we are and who we have the opportunity to be.

We are given the opportunity to experience joy in the face of adversity. Joy in the face of adversity is not that we laugh and celebrate the passing of a loved one or the devastation of a natural disaster but rather the joy in knowing who we truly are. Joy in knowing that all is well and perfect. Knowing that regardless of what life presents we are loved and appreciated beyond measure. Knowing that even though the event that has taken place can cause grief, pain or suffering it benefits us by allowing us to express and experience our Self and therefore the Divine more fully and completely. Being joyful in the face of adversity means we appreciate and accept the goodness of life knowing it is God's Will (our will) for us. In acknowledging and accepting God's Will we know the extent of God's Love. When we express joy in the face of adversity we are empowered and in our empowerment we empower others.

Is it Really by Choice?

Our Souls set specific intentions prior to incarnation. The purpose of these intentions is to facilitate our continuous expansion and expression through the experience of living them out. One would think that because these intentions are set prior to incarnation it is a foregone conclusion that all we have to do is show up and allow them to be played out. However, through the gift of free will we can make any choice in the moment that we want. In other words, we have the ability to make choices, and often do, that are out of alignment with the original intentions our Soul set. The paradox of this is that even though we might make choices that appear to be in conflict with our intentions they are still perfect choices.

How can that be? If a choice is made that is not in alignment with the experience my Soul intended how can that be a perfect choice? Each choice is the perfect choice resulting in the perfect consequences from which to gain what is needed in that moment for our growth and expansion. Each choice offers the opportunity to reflect on and experience who we are and where we are in our growth and expansion in relation to whom and where we desire to be. It is also through this reflection we can *choose again* to realign with the set intentions and therefore live it out.

We can know our Soul's intentions by what we gravitate toward or what resonates most deeply within us. We can know our intentions by what consistently shows up. What are you inspired to do? What excites you the most? What would you do if you knew without a doubt you couldn't fail? What is stirring within you, waiting to be fully expressed?

"Inspirations are nudges from our Soul about something it has a desire to experience and express."

If a choice is contrary to a Soul's intentions but it facilitates a grander expansion, expression and experience of Self, that experience is played out. If however, the Soul's intention is one it absolutely wants to experience in this lifetime it will continue to create opportunities to allow that intention to be experienced.

If the Soul can override a decision what's the point of making decisions or living life in a certain way? If the Soul already knows what it desires to experience through its intentions why would it allow what I might decide or create to be contrary to this desire? Our Soul desires us to have the grandest experience of Self possible in each incarnation through each expression. As a creator on the Earth plane we create experiences through our choices that result in opportunities to express and experience our Self in many ways. If an experience is one that would allow for an expanded experience and expression of Self, then we will have that experience. The whole point of being here in human form is for the grandest experience and expression of Self regardless of where or how that opportunity arises. Whatever is in the highest and best for our Self-expression and experience is what is be played out.I hear questions about the Soul as if it is something distinct and separate from us. You are your Soul. When I say that our Soul is over-riding what we want to do it is actually your higher Self, your Divine essence, that is making the decision, which is another way of saying it is the truth of who you are overriding the illusion of who you believe yourself to be.When you experience circumstances or events that continuously show up they are an indication of an intention looking to be lived out. It is your awareness of the patterns and your understanding of why an event or experience continues to show up that allows you to make conscious choices that would result in the fulfillment of the intention. This is best accomplished by looking at the situation from the perspective of what can be gained from the experience versus why does this keep happening to me.

An example is the type of personal relationships you create with the people that show up in your life. Let's suppose you continuously attract people that do not treat you or love as you would like to be treated. Yet you stay in these relationships beyond what would be considered reasonable. And once one such relationship ends, you find yourself in a new, yet similar, relationship with someone who treats you in the same way.

At first it might seem this new relationship is different and the person acts kindly and lovingly toward you. And then the old pattern sets in. You now find the relationship unfolding in the same manner as the previous one, and the one before that and so on. Your intention with this new relationship wasn't to have the same or similar experience, yet here you are.

What intention do you believe your Soul might have set for this souljourn that would result in one relationship after another that causes emotional pain, suffering, and, in more extreme cases, physical pain? Why would your Soul not provide for the loving relationship and experience you so strongly desire? Keep in mind our Souls don't set intentions that would bring us pain as all intentions from our Soul stem from love and are for the purpose of achieving a grander expression and experience of Self.

In this example, your Soul might have set the intention of experiencing a kind, loving relationship on the Earth plane. However, it is not a kind loving relationship with another person; it is a kind, loving relationship with your Self. The Soul's intention could be that to more fully experience your Self, you are to more fully express love and appreciation toward Self.

The intention is played out perfectly with and through others who offer us the opportunity to love our Self more fully and to make choices in alignment with the experience of self-love and appreciation we desire. The relationships we find ourselves in that are not kind, loving experiences provide the perfect set of circumstances to step away and choose to appreciate, respect and love ourselves as no other can. Once we accept, appreciate, and love our Self in the way we intended we attract others into our lives that reflect that Self-love.

This offers an opportunity to let go of our idea of perfection. For the most part, we see perfection as something exactly as we would like it to be or as we believe it should be. To explain this more fully let's return to the backyard example we used in the description of stepping into uncertainty and expanding our comfort zone.

Here we are again standing on our rear deck looking out on our beautifully manicured lawn and gardens. The grass is mowed to the recommended height; our plants, trees, and shrubs have been trimmed and shaped as we have been told they should be. Everything has been properly fed and fertilized and is spectacular in full bloom and color. But then we notice a few weeds sticking out of one section of our garden. And then we notice a few dandelions beginning to sprout up in our perfectly manicured lawn. Our definition of perfection is when all of the weeds are removed and all plants, trees and shrubs are blooming and trimmed into the form we feel appropriate for the look we desire for our yard. The truth however, is that the weeds we see and the dandelions that are sprouting up are all perfect in their creation. The weed is a perfect weed. The dandelion is a perfect dandelion.

In order for the weed or dandelion to grow, the soil, sunlight, and rain all have to be perfect. It might not be our definition of perfection, however, everything is perfect exactly as it is, regardless of how we think or believe it should be. If it wasn't perfect how could it be?

"Perfection is never what or how we think and believe things should be. Perfection is always as things are."

So it is with our choices, regardless of the choices we make. Even though they might not be what we would consider the perfect choice they will always result in the perfect conditions for our continuous growth, expression, experience, and expansion of Self, our very purpose for being here.

"Everything in and of itself is perfection expressed."

Each souljourn provides the perfect opportunity for our Souls to further experience, express and expand upon themselves as they have intended. In being open, aware and receptive to all life offers we facilitate and perpetuate this process.

Chapter 19

Who Am I?

I came across an advertisement in an airline magazine that had a statement that read, "You are the journey." I saw this as a play on the quote, "It is the journey not the destination." What I understood this to mean was that I, and all other passengers, are the journey for the airline. How the airline meets our needs and expectations is the journey. Their destination might be making a profit. However, if they do not take care of the passengers there will be no profit and the destination will not be reached. And so it is with each of us in our respective lives. If we don't fully embrace the journey, the process of allowing that which we are to be what we express and experience, then our destination, the realization of who we truly are, will not be reached.

What came to mind regarding LIFE as I read the statement in the ad was, "I AM the journey." This was followed immediately by, "I AM the traveler; I AM the vehicle; I AM the destination," which resulted in this full verse.

I AM

I AM the journey; I AM the traveler;
I AM the vehicle; I AM the destination.
I AM the journey,
for it is my relationship with Self that is reflected
to me as my life experiences.
As I AM toward Self; Life is toward me.
I AM the traveler,
as I AM the experience and expression of the Divine;
It is along my life's path that I AM in full
expression of who I AM.
I AM the vehicle.
It is through me the Divine is experienced and expressed.
As I AM in full experience and expression,
the Divine is in full experience and expression.
I AM the destination
for the destination is a return to Self.
I AM That I AM.

This verse means understanding and accepting who I believe myself to be and why I believe I am here. I believe I am an individuated expression of the Divine. I believe my purpose for being is for the Divine to express and experience itself through me on this journey of Self-expression. Living in full expression (LIFE) is the process of allowing that which I Am to be who and what I experience and express during each souljourn.

I believe it is my responsibility, my choice, as to how that expression takes form and is lived out. Therefore, my responsibility is to my Self and how I choose to experience and express my Divinity in any given moment or circumstance. The quality of my life is not determined by what God might shine upon me but on what I shine upon myself. God's love is constant, ever present and without condition. To think that I have to be or act in a certain way to be worthy of God's love is my ego telling me I am not good enough or deserving of God's love just as I am. To withhold love until I act or believe in a certain way is judgment. God is nonjudgmental.

The world returns to me what I believe about my Self. My inner relationship with my Self—your inner relationship with your Self—is what is reflected in the outer world. If what life presents isn't what we desire, we only need look at our relationship with or concept of our Self. It is in honoring, appreciating, nurturing, commending and unconditionally loving our Self that the world responds in kind. It is in loving, honoring, respecting, and appreciating our Self unconditionally that we offer humanity the greatest gift any of us has to offer.

We are all blessed in the same way, not the apparent blessings for which we might express gratitude, such as good health, family, favorable life circumstances, accomplishments or material well-being. We are all blessed in that within each one of us is the power to choose how our Divinity will be experienced through our conscious expression and experience of Self within the context of life's events.

Who Sees What I See?

Within all of us is the understanding and knowing of whom we truly are. Not the physical body we see, not the thoughts we hold about who we think we are, and certainly not the labels we give ourselves or that others might place on us. There is this knowing that there is something much more than what we see and experience as our physical selves. Most people with whom I speak agree there is something within and beyond themselves they feel or know, but can't quite explain or describe. It is a detachment from everything and yet a connection to all things. There is no beginning or end, just continuation and expansiveness. Imagine your Self not being. You can't because you always have been and will be.

How do you answer these questions:

Who or what is looking out at the world from behind my eyes?

Who or what is aware I AM looking out from behind these eyes?

Who or what is aware of being aware of what is seen from these eyes?

These are intriguing and thought provoking questions, don't you think? Asking them of your Self will give you a greater awareness of the Truth of who you are. You will come to know you are not your body; you are the presence within the body.

I AM Who I AM,
always have been and will be.

Who I Am is Who I AM
and will not change.

It is who I believe my Self to be
that changes to reflect Who I AM
so I AM who I AM.

A phrase that helps me better understand this experience of detachment and connectedness is, "*giving into the moment.*" I see and have a sense of one thing collapsing into another. It is a folding in or accepting of one thing for another only to become one and the same. A wave in the ocean building up to the point when it can no longer sustain itself only to collapse back into that from which it arose. Even though the wave is always a part of the ocean we see it and perhaps experience it as somehow separate.

Giving into the moment feels like this to me. It is allowing things (thoughts) in the form of stresses, struggles and fears which I have allowed to build to the point where I cannot or am no longer willing to sustain them to collapse into the nothingness from which I created them.

"Giving into the moment is surrender, but it is not giving up. It is a collapsing of all things into the one of which we are all a part."

So what is the experience that causes the buildup that leads to the collapse? In the simplest of terms, as I have mentioned before, it is our resistance to life. It is resistance to living in full expression. It is our fight against the flow of what is being offered for our continued growth and expansion. The more we resist, the more complex our lives. The more complex we make our lives, the more we struggle. We resist because we *think* we know what is best for us instead of allowing, accepting and embracing what life is offering. We are not trusting in Life, and we are not trusting in Self. Life always presents what we need when we need it whether we recognize it as such or not.

Think to a time when you told a lie. As time went on it became more and more difficult to sustain. It was hard to remember what and to whom it was said. Layer upon layer was placed on the original lie the more times it was told. As a result, other things happened or came into play that added to the original lie. It became more difficult and more stressful to uphold.

This is what is happening to all of us during our lifetimes. We lie to our Self and others about who we are. We are constantly working to live up to an idea or image of who we and others believe ourselves to be in spite of the knowing in our hearts it is not who we truly are. Our struggle in life is the extraordinary effort required to maintain that lie.

Giving into the moment is the letting go of the lie we have been living to allow our true Self to be experienced and expressed. It is a settling into our Self, that comfortable, familiar place that takes no effort, no thought, just being, just allowing. Settling into our Self is embracing what life offers in every moment. It is accepting the part we play in the co-creation of the opportunities, many times disguised as struggle, that are for our grandest experience and expression of Self.

"Trust in the simple flow of life in the present moment."

I know I resist life. I try to make things happen the way I think they should within the time frame I think they should. Throughout my life this has and to this day continues to cause great stress and frustration. And yet, it is in those times that I give into the moment, when I let go of the need to control the situation, that I am reminded I need do nothing except allow life to flow to and through me in the way it is intended.

My life experiences will come to me because they are just that, my life experiences; they belong to no one else. All I have to do is be aware of and embrace my life as it unfolds beautifully, naturally and effortlessly. It always, in all ways, unfolds for my benefit. Have FAITH, fully allow it to happen.

An interesting aspect of this process of life (living in full expression) is that even though we are co-creators in the experiences/opportunities life presents, we always have the choice to participate or not in that which we have co-created. This now begs the question as to why we would resist that which we have co-created that is perfectly designed for our continued spiritual growth and expansion. Why are we even given the gift of choice in such an important matter? Because it is in choosing how we desire to experience and express our Self that we exercise our power as a creator. Every choice presents a new opportunity for another expression and experience of how powerful a creator we are.

Our perfectly designed plan is not set in stone but the outcome is. Everyone eventually gets back to the Source where we began, regardless of the many detours we chose to take. The path we choose to "recover" who we truly are is up to each one of us. Each step we take, where ever our foot falls, opens the way for life to unfold perfectly as intended. There is no right or wrong step. Each step is an opportunity for experiencing and expressing who we are in that moment.

"There is no right path or wrong path,
there is your path."

To be who we know our Self to be is to allow the greatness and the glory that is within each one of us to be fully expressed. It is in these moments when we allow our greatness to be expressed and experienced that life flows to and through us effortlessly, naturally and beautifully. The more we give into these moments, the more of these moments we are given.

"There is within each moment the potential,
the opportunity and the responsibility,
to change the world for the better

through our grandest expression and experience of Self."

LIFE is singing the song that yearns to be sung. We all have one; in fact, we are the song that yearns to be sung. We can feel it; we know it exists; but we might not know exactly what it is or what to do with it. I assure you it is within you; it is in all of us, perhaps as an uneasiness, an uncertainty, a knowing, or even a sense that something of great magnitude is about to take place. Our song is the grandest expression and experience of Self. It patiently awaits our willingness to sing loud and clear.

Final Thoughts

As you set this book aside, perhaps for a moment, perhaps for the final time, it is my sincere desire that it has brought about greater awareness. Out of awareness comes greater understanding and wisdom. Awareness allows love, peace, joy and happiness to be experienced and expressed, even in the face of adversity. Awareness is consciousness; we are consciousness. Awareness allows the grandest experience and expression of Self.

"We are at first aware, then awareness itself."

Live in full expression of who you are and the Divine is in full expression. Be faithful to and trust in Self. Live in gratitude for all that life is and all that life offers.

As you awaken each morning, simply ask, "What experience and expression of Self do I desire today? What is required of me today to live in full expression of the truth of who I AM?"

I wish you safe travels on this and subsequent souljourns. Be the blessing you desire in the world and you will be likewise blessed.

Jim

The Lord's Prayer

Translated from its original Aramaic by Dr. Rocco Errico
Our Father who is everywhere
Your name is sacred.
Your kingdom is come.
Your will is throughout the earth
even as it is throughout the universe
You give us our needful bread from day to day,
And you forgive us our offenses
even as we forgive our offenders.
And you let us not enter into materialism.
But you separate us from error.
Because yours are the kingdom, the power and the song and praise.
From all ages, throughout all ages.
(Sealed) in faith, trust and truth.

About the Author

Jim Phillips is an author, speaker and certified L.I.F.E., spiritual and business coach. For the better part of 30 years he has been an entrepreneur and business leader inspiring others to higher levels of achievement and understanding through his coaching, writing and presentations. His true passion is the exploration and application of spiritual law as it applies to prosperity and overall quality of life. One of Jim's gifts is his ability to help others understand and apply complex spiritual concepts to their personal life which has resulted in their creating and experiencing more of who they truly are and what they desire from life.

At the age of thirteen Jim had a profound experience that confirmed he had a very specific message to share about our connection to the Divine and our Divinity. This message was to be shared when the time was right. That time is now. Never has there been a time in the history of humanity when there was a greater need to understand who we are and why we are here. Never has there been a time in the history of humanity when there have been more people open and receptive to this message.

Jim was born in Buffalo, New York, however he lived the majority of his childhood years in Virginia. He graduated from James Madison University with a degree in Business Administration and Management. Jim currently resides in Aldie, VA where he continues his writing, coaching and speaking. You can reach Jim at www.livinginfullexpression.com

CPSIA information can be obtained
at www.ICGtesting.com
Printed in the USA
FFOW03n2118150217
32398FF